AFTERthree

Know...Walk...Respond

Dr. Ben Gutierrez

Academx
Publishing Services

Printed in the United States of America

ISBN-10: 1-60036-188-9

ISBN-13: 978-1-60036-188-3

To Dr. Ron Hawkins
A distinguished colleague who has encouraged me in my
writing & research. A dedicated husband & father who has
been an inspiration to me to balance life, family, and ministry.
A devoted believer in Christ who has exemplified a passion for
God's Word & personal holiness. And a dear friend.
Thank you.

ACKNOWLEDGEMENTS

This page serves to recognize the myriad of support I received in writing this book. Without whose help, I would not have been able to complete this very satisfying task.

Thank you to my wife, Tammy, whose support and encouragement through the ups and downs of life keep me going and enthused to continue to minister. I love you.

Thank you to my precious daughters, Lauren Ashton & Emma Jordan, who fill my life with such joy and laughter. I pray I live out the truths taught in this book every day before you. I love you both so much.

To Jill Walker, your acute attention to detail in managing the editing process of this book has been unparalleled. Your professionalism, knowledge of the process, and flexible spirit has been the most critical factor in the completion of this book. Without your contribution, this book could not have been completed. Many thanks!

To Sharon Harrington, thank you for your countless hours of editing and your ability to pay such close attention to smallest detail. It is your insight that has brought such great readability to this project.

To Leigh Germy, the publishing world's "Best Kept Secret". Now that I have announced it to the world, my hope is that you're no longer a secret! I pray you will reserve your time in the future to join with me in future projects. Thank you very much for your excellent work. Leigh can be reached at www.leighgermy.com.

To the leadership of Liberty University & Thomas Road Baptist Church, who provide for me the richest environments in which to edify the body of Christ. Thank you for your encouragement to write, teach, administrate, lead, and dream big. There is no better place to live, work, and minister than on Liberty Mountain!

Table of Contents

✓

THE QUESTIONS

As a Christian, I always knew the basic tenets of the Christian faith. As a pastor, I always inserted a presentation of salvation in every sermon. But it wasn't until I became a parent that I began to feel a literal burning in my soul that moved me to articulate the truths of how someone can receive eternal salvation.

It wasn't that I lacked passion, was careless with my presentation or that I ever shared incorrect or incomplete information prior to becoming a parent – not at all. But when you look into the brilliant blue eyes of your gorgeous miracle that God has given you, and realize that this horrible thing called "sin" will attack her little soul with zero care for how it will utterly disturb and destroy her life; I felt an exorbitant sense of urgency to be able to articulate the truth that can set her free from the power of sin in this life, and provide a hope of forever being with the Savior of her soul. Very early on in her life, I wanted her to learn the ways of her Savior and lean on this God Who so beautifully knitted her in her mother's womb (Psalm 139:13-14).

I liken this urgency for my own child's eternal state to a parent who can watch 100 little neighborhood girls practice for gymnastics in a large gym, knowing there is only one special child in that large gym that consumes the parent's focus and attention. Of course, you care for the well-being of the other children - when other children fall off of a balance beam, you don't hesitate to alert their parent of the fall. But your child receives additional care and counsel from you regarding how to be safe. You caution them it in the car ride to the gym. You remind them during workout breaks. And, of course, another rehearsal of all you told them on the way home from practice never hurts. These cautions are added to the myriad of daily warnings you offer your child about all other dangerous possibilities in the world (i.e. pinching your fingers in the front door, running on the slick wood floors with just your socks on, etc). But WHY does a parent go this far and to this extreme to caution their child about every ill that could befall him/her? Because it's YOUR child!

This book comes out of my feeling of immediate urgency and immense care that I have for those with whom I interact and those that I may never meet. The urgency is for everyone, regardless of age, to have a clear, concise explanation of their need for a Savior and to understand the incomparable invitation by God to enter into an intimate relationship with Him.

I am persuaded that these purposes are issues of every person's heart and a true seeker of truth longs to know how these principles can become a reality in his/her own life. From the moment I began my teaching and pastoring career, I have experienced parishioner after parishioner, and student after student ask me the same questions. No matter where I was ministering and regardless of the ministry leadership position, members of the Body of Christ approached me with the same questions. The questions would come after preaching a sermon, at the church altar, hallway conversations in the university, Q&A discussion in a symposium, email communiqués, and phone calls. The questions are:

"How do I know I am saved?"
"How can I grow in my intimacy with God?"

After hearing these questions time & time again, it did not take me long before I found myself saying, "I need to write this down so that I can simply forward to anyone who asks me in the future." So, I was convinced that my very well-rehearsed response should be put on paper. And finally, that day has come in the form of this book.

I pray that God will speak to you through the reading of this book and that you will be surprised by both the unconditional love that the Creator of the world has for you individually and how you can express a great appreciation for Who He is and all He has done for you by cultivating a strong desire to honor him with your life.

I invite you to join me on this spiritual journey.

Ben Gutierrez

KNOW

CHAPTER ONE

Know Who You Are

When I was young, I remember my father asking me to go fishing with him at a larger state park down the highway a few miles. At that time, I loved to go fishing and immediately took him up on his invitation. We got our equipment out of the car, walked down the grassy hill to a semi-hidden portion of the lake, and we began to 'wet a line'. On one particular trip, I specifically recall catching a ton of catfish. They were biting like crazy! They were biting so well that it seemed like they were on our lines before the cast ever made it into the water. It was a great day.

When we filled the entire cooler with catfish, my father told me to make sure the cooler had fresh water for them to breathe and keep them alive during our 30-minute drive home. Right then, I asked my father what seemingly to me was a very simple question to answer. I asked, "Dad, how do fish breathe under water?"

"Well, that's a good question, son" He said. And for the first time, my father who in my eyes knew every answer to every question about everything began to stumble in his explanation. I remember he said, "Well, they pass water through their gills, you see?" as he pointed to one fish in the cooler. "Yeah Dad, I see, but how do they breathe air?" "Uh, well, they don't...but the water passes through their gills and there are air molecules in the water that they pick up through their gills, you see?" as he once again pointed to a different fish in the cooler. "Ok, Dad, I see their gills moving, but I thought you had to hold your breath under water because you can't breathe under water, right?"

What started as a very simple question turned into a very detailed and intricate conversation. Even though my Father had a difficult time explaining the intricacies of how fish breathe under water, there was no doubt it was happening as evidenced by the catfish staring up at us watching us ponder these truths.

3

The same scenario seems to play out when pondering spiritual questions as well. When people begin asking questions about spiritual issues – *"What exactly is salvation?" "Does everyone need to be saved?" "If so, saved from what?" "How did things get this way?"* – What seems like simple questions are, at times, somewhat difficult to explain, even though the reality of each one is plainly evidenced in the lives of every person. But the possibility of these questions causing confusion ought not to keep people from discussing them.

These questions are necessary to ultimate peace in the human soul, and to have full enlightenment of how one's soul can experience true peace, a thoughtful and biblical response must be carefully understood.

Questions about salvation have been on peoples' hearts and minds for thousands of years. In Acts 16, we read of a jailer who had been asked to detain the Apostle Paul and Silas in prison for proclaiming the good news of salvation provided through Jesus Christ. In the middle of the night, the jailer, along with the other prisoners, was stunned to hear singing, expressions of joy, and a level of enthusiasm that the jailer was not accustomed to witnessing, especially from two prisoners who had been publicly beaten and detained for their personal religious beliefs. This unexpected enthusiasm must have puzzled the jailer, and I wonder if he may have mentally engaged in the message of the songs that were being sung by these two passionate Christian captives.

As you read you will note that at midnight God miraculously liberated the singing prisoners and their fellow inmates with an earthquake that caused all the prison doors to open and the shackles to fall off. The jailer, amazed at the hand of God and grateful that the prisoners had not escaped, was led to ask a pressing spiritual question, a question that was weighing on his heart. He ran back into the prison and bowed before Paul and Silas asking, "Sirs, what must I do to be saved?"

Paul's response to the jailer is one simple statement, "Believe in the Lord Jesus Christ and you will be saved."

What Does It Mean To Be Saved?

This is a very important question – one that has both spiritual and eternal consequences. Using the Word of God, we will answer these questions in this chapter.

It is interesting that the Bible rarely provides a full teaching of every concept of a doctrine within one verse or paragraph. Rather, the Bible disperses the full teaching of a particular doctrine within a number of related verses. As a result, one will not receive a full, clear teaching of a biblical concept until he reads and processes all the verses related to a particular scriptural topic. This is the approach we will take in our journey through the Bible in search of a full and clear teaching of salvation. It may seem like an insurmountable task but don't be discouraged. I promise that it can and will be a life-changing journey for you. I pray you will be able to reserve some uninterrupted time to sit down to read and consider the scriptures we will be looking at which speak profound, yet easily understandable truths that promise to change your life forever.

Perfect clarity is needed in order to cognitively know the facts and volitional requirements of salvation needed to come to a saving knowledge of Jesus Christ.

To begin with, every Christian needs to stand firmly on the biblical truth that Jesus is the only way to salvation.

Let's Take a Look

Knowing that the following verses are taken from the very Word of God, let's be patient and careful as we gratefully look at the following biblical passages, which will either confirm our already-established salvation or offer guidance on how we can recieve eternal life and peace with God.

Romans 3:23 teaches that we are spiritually lost and in need of salvation. *"For all have sinned and fall short of the glory of God."*

This verse clearly teaches us that all mankind is lost. Every person needs to be saved because every person is spiritually lost. And, unlike being lost in a forest where you may find your way out, the state of spiritual lostness cannot be remedied by human means. Why? Because it is our very nature to sin.

Our souls are not lost because of the sins that we have committed. We commit sins because of our nature or sinful state. Unfortunately, we often hear folks share the gospel by saying, "You must be forgiven for the bad things you have done." No. Our souls are condemned because of our sinful state. When believers share the gospel, they typically refer to the fact that the listener has sinned, but the listener must be led to understand that we commit sinful acts because we have a sinful heart and out of that sinful core we manifest our true nature. Even though a person may not feel they are a sinner in need of salvation, the truth is they are. One's need for salvation is based on this truth and it is crucial to convey this truth to nonbelievers.

In our society, most people don't like being lumped in the same category with murderers and kidnappers, and they see things like cheating on taxes, swearing, or telling little white lies as not so serious. But to God, sin is sin because it is a manifestation of what is at the very core of our being. If our gauge for holiness is to compare ourselves with other human beings, I am sure we could all find at least ten people who we would compare to very well. But the Bible teaches us that the gauge is God's holiness, the perfect glory of God, and a standard far beyond our ability to reach.

Romans 6:23 teaches that we deserve to be punished because of having a sinful heart.
"For the wages of sin is death, but the gift of God is eternal life in Christ Jesus our Lord."

Because of our sinful state, we have earned God's holy wrath. Our culpability for our sin is likened to how we expect to receive a paycheck after we complete a job from an employer. Once we have performed our job, we expect and deserve to be paid. Another example would be a criminal who is caught for committing a crime deserving his sentence to prison. Because of our sinful state, because we have "fallen short of His glory," all of the souls of humankind deserve to be judged by God and receive a guilty verdict from Him. And, upon receiving this verdict, the human soul is promised to be the recipient of a very tough, yet deserved, sentence ... unless we can find Someone who is able to take upon Himself the penalty for our sinfulness and satisfy the judgment of God and release us from having to pay the penalty ourselves. The exciting truth is that this is indeed possible, but first you must conclude that there is no possible way you can personally pay your own sin penalty.

Isaiah 64:6a teaches that prior to salvation, even our best deeds or intentions are inneffective to save, and thus any attempt to save our own souls is repulsive to God.
"But we are all like an unclean thing, and all our righteousness are like filthy rags..."

Our righteousness, or good behavior, is as "filthy rags" in God's eyes. This means that every attempt to achieve salvation on our own is impossible. Every good deed, charitable action, thought, or even our sincere pursuit and intention, is unclean and unacceptable. To think that we could merit salvation by our own efforts is nauseating and offensive to the God Who is the only One able to provide a sufficient payment for our sin.

Even though an unsaved person can perform charitable deeds and express kindness that reflects Christianity, at best he is performing those actions while wallowing in a sinful state, a realm that is offensive to God. Therefore, it is not the actions that save, but the change of heart behind the actions that is required.

Unfortunately, sometimes people don't even know they are living a life that is offensive to God. They never realize that regardless of their culturally approved, or sometimes even church approved lifestyle, if their sinful state has never been addressed through God's forgiveness and cleansing, these actions come from a heart that is repulsive to God. For example, it would be the same as accepting the words, "I'm sorry, please forgive me" from a person who was in the middle of plotting their second attempt to steal your belongings. The words, if devoid of context, sound good but they are not backed up by a heart that is pure and clean. Again, it is our sinful state that has earned us God's wrath and judgment and any "cleaning up" of our actions, words, or deeds without experiencing true heart change is, in effect, futile and powerless because it is done from a heart that is an offense to God.

Titus 3:5 teaches that there is no possible way to obtain salvation by actions, thoughts, or good deeds that we can do, think, or perform.
"Not by works of righteousness which we have done, but according to His mercy He saved us, through the washing of regeneration and renewing of the Holy Spirit."

This verse illustrates that there is only One who provides the cleansing of our sinful state – God Himself in the form of the Holy Spirit. We have seen that we cannot save ourselves and that we need God to save us. It is all about what God does in this one-sided process for us. This is further developed in Matthew 5:3:

Matthew 5:3 teaches that we cannot bring anything of spiritual value in and of ourselves to the table that could positively persuade God to establish peace with Him apart from receiving His forgiveness.
"Blessed are the poor in spirit, for theirs is the kingdom of heaven."

When we approach the spiritual "bargaining table" with God regarding our salvation, it is actually a place where we simply plead with Him for His grace and mercy. There is actually no bargaining at all in this one-sided arbitration. We cannot approach Him and say: "Let me remind you who my parents were," or, "Here is my stellar history of community service," or "Here are all of my accomplishments." There is literally nothing that we can put on the table that can entice God to say, "Wow! Now this guy really lived a great life. If anyone deserves heaven, it should be him!" On the contrary, Matthew 5:3 teaches that if you want to enter into the Kingdom of God, you must acknowledge that you are "poor in spirit," no matter what you have accomplished in your life.

What is interesting is that, in the original language of the New Testament (called "koine Greek" pronounced "*COIN-ay*"), there were actually two words for the word "poor" that the Holy Spirit could have chosen to describe one's spiritual state in Matthew 5:3. One of the words is the word *penichros* (pronounced *PENny-cross*) which means that someone is "needy" or "poor." This would refer to someone who has some possessions but needs additional things to add to his collection of possessions (e.g. you have a car, but need gas; you have a house, but need food; etc). But that is not the word that is translated "poor" in Matthew 5:3.

The word for "poor" in Matthew 5:3 is the word "*Ptokos*" (Pronounced "p-toe-COSS") which means "totally destitute" or "utterly impoverished." This word is used to describe someone who literally has *absolutely nothing*. This same word is used in the Gospel of Luke to describe a beggar who is extending his arms asking for alms on a street corner. Being incredibly ashamed of his destitute state, he chooses to hide his face in shame as he pleads for alms (Luke 18).

Therefore, Matthew 5:3 teaches that the one who approaches God and receives salvation has nothing to offer God in his attempt to persuade God to save him. The individuals who will inherit eternal life are those who come to God recognizing and acknowledging that they have nothing to change their sinful state and understand that, without God's intervention, they ought to be the recipient of punishment.

As a professor, I have no greater joy than to watch students grow academically, socially, physically, and spiritually. There are some students I tend to interact with more than others as a result of being enrolled in a particular training program. It is with these students that I have more occasion to do life with. Throughout the years, we interact formally in the classroom and informally in the office or hallway and we flush out various issues, decisions, and challenges. Most of the time, these conversations are positive and amicable but sometimes a conversation may be prescriptive or involve a soft reproof due to a recent poor choice or action taken by the student. It is never easy to confront a student and talk about poor choices that the student might have made, but it is all a part of demonstrating to the student that I sincerely care for their well being, character, and testimony.

I recall a new professor who joined our university faculty who once asked me about how to strike the right balance in the professor-student relationship, and how to balance having a friendship with the student while at the same time reserving the right to correct the student if necessary. I responded by describing how God deals with us as His children.

God loves us and wants the best for us. He lovingly maintains a standard of personal righteousness that is required of every person, and He will not lower this standard because that would be a lie and not what is best for the person. Likewise, we as professors must confront only when necessary always asking ourselves what is the best piece of advice for this student.

Then I told him that the way you know you have struck the right balance is when, at the end of their academic career, you have that bitter-sweet feeling of joy and sadness when you see them walk across the stage and celebrate the completion of one phase of their life, knowing you have poured your life into them, wishing you could have done more, but thankful for the rich times you experienced together.

I instructed the new professor on one more scenario that he might come up against when a student he knows well comes up to him and admits guilt and responsibility for a wrong doing without making excuses or trying to hide the truth. I advised him it is at that point you want to show the student mercy and try to work with him, because in his heart he understands and acceps both the weight of his actions and the value of the mercy you will show him.

That is exactly what our Lord requires of us as we approach Him understanding that we are "poor in spirit". Understanding our guilt and our inability to rectify it, we then and only then understand the true value of the mercy God lavishes upon us.

Ephesians 2:8-9 teaches that no person is able to boast about how they are able to save their own soul because salvation is made available in the form of a gift from God to all who desire to receive His salvation.
"For by grace you have been saved through faith, and that not of yourselves; it is the gift of God, not of works, lest anyone should boast."

The Bible teaches that God invites anyone to accept His free gift. This gift or sufficient payment cannot and is not found within the power or abilities of the person who stands in need of salvation. This payment for sin does not spring forth from a heart that is tainted with sin. You cannot change your spiritual state by some deed or physical act. The best deed in man's eyes, and done with even the purest of intentions, will never be able to change his spiritual state of sinfulness.

It is impossible to change your spiritual state by physical means. I liken it to an occasion when a person gets emotionally depressed and just sits in front of the television or eats a gallon of ice cream to appease their deep-seated pain. The TV and ice cream may provide a temporary getaway from one's problems, but they certainly don't confront the root of these problems. Even Judas Iscariot, after betraying Jesus Christ and feeling a deep emotional regret, went back to the Sanhedrin and tried to return the thirty pieces of silver in an attempt to appease his condemned conscience but his attempt was futile (Matthew 27:3-5). Regardless of how much we would want to save our own soul, we cannot change our spiritual state ourselves. Therefore, we cannot brag to others that we had any part in our salvation. "It is by grace you have been saved through faith," meaning through trust and total dependence on God to save you. Salvation cannot be produced from within ourselves; it is a gift that only God can give you.

According to Ephesians 2:8-9, the payment for one's sin must come from a source that is holy, righteous, and absent of any sin whatsoever. It logically follows that the gift of salvation must come from the only One who is able to produce a pure gift to appease His judgment: God Himself. Therefore, the One before Whom we stand before in a guilty and sinful state is the same One we plead with to be merciful to us, to forgive us, and to extend His grace and divine mercy to us.

Romans 5:8 teaches that God extended an invitation for you to enter into a peaceful relationship with Him.
"But God demonstrates His own love toward us, in that while we were still sinners, Christ died for us."

Notice that this verse begins with the word "but," contrasting any notion that we can save ourselves. This verse offers hope but not before we conclude that our soul is utterly lost and guilty in God's eyes. Prior to offering hope, this verse accentuates the impossibility of saving our own souls.

By now, have you noticed that the Bible wants to drive home the state of our lostness? Why is this? Probably because the degree to which we understand the depth of our lostness determines the degree to which we will value the gift of salvation that allows us to have peace with God. By understanding what the Bible teaches about our hopelessness without Christ, we realize that our souls need a merciful God to intervene in order to provide us the gift of salvation that we are unable to provide for ourselves.

It is indeed a scary thing to know that, aside from God's intervention, we would forever remain in our sinful state that results in eternal judgment. 1 John 1:5 says, *"In him there is light, there is no darkness at all."* As long as we have a sinful heart that has not been forgiven by God, we cannot commune with our Creator, the God of heaven and earth. We cannot have an intimate relationship with Him. We may be generally aware that there is a "higher being" that is more powerful than we are, and we may even try to talk to Him from time to time, but we really can't have a personal relationship with Him until our sinfulness is dealt with.

Romans 5:8 adds an interesting glimpse into the gracious heart of God found in the phrase, "while we were yet sinners." The Lord Jesus Christ provided a payment for our sin even when we had no idea that we were sinners. Before we came to our senses spiritually, He had his hand extended to offer salvation for our sin. This is what should cause our hearts to grieve over a world of people who mock His name. They are completely unaware of what Jesus went through for them and do not realize that He is offering full salvation if they would only believe in Him and receive His free gift. It is sobering to know there are people walking around today that have physical, economical, familial, or political peace, but not peace in their soul through Jesus Christ. People's souls do not receive punishment because of a lack of an invitation to receive that peace, but because they will not accept Christ's payment for sin.

Romans 10:9-10 teaches that if we want to accept Christ, we must respond in TWO ways.
"That if you confess with your mouth the Lord Jesus and believe in your heart that God has raised Him from the dead, you will be saved. For with the heart one believes unto righteousness, and with the mouth confession is made unto salvation."

This passage teaches us that we must respond in two ways. Responding in one way without responding in the other way does not result in salvation. Before we can confess with our mouth the Lord Jesus, we must first have a cognitive understanding of four facts:

1. Agree with God regarding your sinful state
We must be in agreement that our sinful state merits judgment and spiritual death. We must concede that we deserve to pay the penalty for our sin.

2. Believe that Jesus is God
We have to believe that Jesus is 100% God because if Jesus is just some man then He is humanly unable to offer salvation. If He's just a good teacher then He is unable to offer forgiveness of sins through His salvation. If this were true, He could only point you to a way of salvation rather than saying, *"I am the way, the truth, and the life. No one comes to the Father except through Me."* (John 14:6).

3. Believe that Jesus' sacrifice was the only sufficient sacrifice to atone for your sin

We must believe that Jesus' sacrifice is sufficient in totality, and is able to provide atonement for our sin. Atonement means to cover by virtue of providing a payment. Sufficient means that the atonement was not only paid in full but was the only payment possible to fully pay for our sin. In other words, we don't need anything else. Jesus Christ's death on the cross and resurrection are totally adequate to atone for our sins, and for our sin debt.

Again, the reason why Jesus had to die on the cross was because our sin-debt needed to be paid for. Someone was required to pay the price. Without Jesus, we are compelled to pay this eternal price ourselves. Prior to accepting Jesus Christ's payment for my sin, I was the one who, upon death, would have been called upon to pay for my sin. However, I applied Jesus Christ's payment to my heart and received his salvation, allowing Him to pay the sin debt that I owed.

4. Believe that Jesus physically rose from the dead, thereby proving that He can conquer both physical and spiritual death.

Romans 10:9-10 says, *"that if you confess with your mouth the Lord Jesus and believe in your heart that God has raised Him from the dead, you will be saved. For with the heart one believes unto righteousness, and with the mouth confession is made unto salvation."*

In our finite human minds, we may not have a problem believing that Jesus lived or forgives sins, but it may seem difficult to fathom that Jesus Christ also arose from the dead. Fortunately, the truth of His resurrection is clearly taught and concretely defendable. In order to accept God's offer of salvation, we must believe fully that Jesus physically rose from the dead, and is alive and well in Heaven today.

Just Knowing Isn't Everything

Like I said at the outset, sometimes seemingly "simple" questions are weighted with great significance and meaning – especially questions that deal with issues of spirituality, one's soul, and the need to have true peace with God. This chapter has served to provide a straightforward explanation of some spiritual questions that everyone must answer in his/her life. Fortunately, the Bible offers some clear answers to these important questions. There is more to this spiritual discussion though.

There is more to this spiritual discussion though.

Now that we know exactly what salvation is, it is equally important to know what it is not. Salvation is not just a matter of cognitive knowledge – it alone is not enough. We'll discuss this further in the next chapter.

write It Down

What one Bible verse really struck you as profound or suprising as you read this chapter? Why?

_____

_____

_____

_____

_____

_____

_____

_____

_____

_____

_____

_____

_____

_____

_____

_____

Reflect on your salvation story (if applicable) and spend some time writing about when you came to a cognitive knowledge of Who Jesus Christ is and what He has done for you. If you are not yet a believer, spend some time writing down reasons why you are not a believer right now. Write down your thoughts about what this chapter taught you about becoming a believer.

_____

_____

_____

_____

_____

_____

_____

_____

_____

_____

_____

_____

_____

_____

_____

_____

_____

Notes

CHAPTER TWO

Know Whose You Are

This may surprise you – for sure it shocked me when I personally contemplated the thought – but the more I searched the Scriptures, I realized that the Scriptures make a very distinct difference between simply knowing facts only, and knowing facts about God along with knowing the God of the facts.

You may have read the previous chapter's cognitive facts and got excited about these great truths, but the key question, however, is this, "*What makes true belief in Jesus Christ any different from demons who acknowledge the exact same four cognitive facts about Jesus Christ?*"

In the book of James, the Bible says, "Even the demons believe—and tremble!" (James 2:19b). Further, in Mark 1:24 we see that demons believe every single fact I have listed. There was one encounter where the demons came to Jesus while they possessed an individual and they said, "What business do we have with each other, Jesus of Nazareth? Have You come to destroy us? I know who You are the Holy One of God!" I would actually like to get some church members to say something like that on occasion. We know biblically that demons can never be saved because they are forever against Christ. They hate Christ and do everything possible to thwart the plan of Christ. But they believe cognitively every single fact we have listed about Jesus Christ. Demons believe that He is God and they believe that Jesus Christ's sacrifice was indeed sufficient to save sins. They also believe He rose from the dead. In fact, they probably know a whole lot more about Scripture and believe it more than some Christians do it seems.

So, what completes the process beyond our knowledge? What is enough? After you die and you stand before God, what will you say when He asks you, "Why should I let you into my heaven?" If you count off the four things we have mentioned so far in this book, God will then ask you one more question, "The demons believe those same facts, but they can never be saved nor be the recipient of my eternal life. So if they believe these facts and they are not saved, what is the difference between them and you?" How would you answer? Would you know what the difference is and be able to express it to God as you stand in awe before Him?

The answer: A person must know the truths of Christ *cognitively* and believe them *volitionally!*

Believing volitionally is an act of the will and it is total dependence and trust in Jesus Christ. Willingly invite God to infuse your heart, which is the center of your decision-making force, with His purpose, truth, and conviction. It is not belief in a creed or a mere belief system, but total trust is placed in the Person of Jesus Christ. It must be more than the acknowledgement that demons give Jesus Christ. The difference should be the heart's love and commitment to have Jesus as a welcomed ruler of their souls.

This is evidenced in Romans 10:9-10 where we see that when we accept Christ we are responding in two ways. The second way is volitionally -- an act of the will. When we say that we "ask Christ in our heart," what does that really mean? When the heart is referenced in Scripture it is often this way, "as a man thinks in his heart so is he" or "out of the abundance of the heart the mouth speaks." It's a mistake, biblically and exegetically, to say that the heart is the emotion and the mind is the intellect, because often in the Old Testament the heart is coupled with words that denote thinking. When you speak of the heart, or when you accept Christ, it is more than a cognitive action, more than credence — it is dependence and full trust in Him. We literally ask and call on Christ to infuse our lives, our hearts and our thoughts with His will. That's why Jesus in John 10:27 says that a great evidence of salvation is this, "My sheep hear My voice, and I know them, and they follow Me." Christians will not always have full agreement on all doctrines, but I know one thing; a person's good deeds or charitable actions will not save him; however, words, deeds, trust, and attitude are all great evidences that you have accepted Christ. When you are saved, your life reflects dependence on Christ and commitment to His Word. You may not know everything as a believer, but you have that passion to grow.

How do you know you believe volitionally? At the moment of requesting salvation, the heart will experience these realities:

Your heart will have remorse over sin.
In Matthew 5, the Beatitudes passage, we read, "Blessed are they who mourn." After you realize that you are poor in spirit, you begin to mourn; it makes perfect, logical sense. We have remorse, not just because we are caught or enslaved by sin, but because we truly feel remorse over our sin and our sinful

state. We feel ashamed of our sin and because of our lifestyle, we want to change our spiritual condition. And through this remorse we see our need for a perfect God.

Your heart will repent for your sin.
Repentance is more than feeling bad. Repentance is turning and running, going in another direction. You are literally grieved and that grief has turned your heart to run to what is right and holy. Will we be tempted to turn around and consider our old ways? Unfortunately, yes. But there will always be some level of conviction following sin that is wrong and contrary to our newly forgiven nature.

You will request salvation from sin.
Our prayer is this; "I don't want my sinful state anymore. I don't want to function out of a state that is offensive to You, Holy God. Would You change me and would You give me the power to overcome sin in my life?" We see here the difference between credence and dependence. We are not just cognitively depending on Christ, but volitionally. You cannot have one without the other. You could say, "Sure, I'll depend and trust on Christ. He's a great guy and might make my life better." But there is no hope in such a philosophy. We cannot give this type of message to people who are suffering in the Middle East, or in the 10/40 Window, or in sub-Saharan Africa because their lives will not be impacted by such a message. You can't just willingly say, "I'll trust Him" without knowing what you believe or even what you are saved from.

Last chapter, we examined where every person stands in relationship with their Creator -- how exactly one can be forgiven of their sin and have an intimate relationship with God. And even though we covered a lot of detail, it may be helpful to talk about what salvation is NOT in order to solidify our understanding of salvation.

One technique to fully understanding a concept is to examine the exact opposite and by contrast you will gain a better understanding of the original concept. For example, there is a verse in the Bible that has confused many people throughout the years. It is a verse that teaches that we should be "filled with the Spirit". Some have asked, "Ok, but what does being filled with the Spirit actually mean?" And as you can see, the verse doesn't offer an explanation of what this phrase means but rather offers a contrasting comparison in order to understand the command to "Be filled with the Spirit." Here's what Ephesians 5:18 says:

"And do not be drunk with wine, in which is dissipation; but be filled with the Spirit"

"Be filled" must be the opposite concept of "being drunk". So, to understand what being drunk implies, we can better understand what it means to "be filled with the Spirit." The comparison is simple. Just as wine controls a person, makes them do disgraceful things, affects their thinking and actions; likewise, the believer ought to be controlled by the Holy Spirit. The Holy Spirit should control every thought and action. The Holy Spirit should so affect the mind of the believer that the believer defaults to Christ-like thoughts, actions/reactions, and passions. By studying the opposite concept, we have a more vivid understanding of what the verse is saying.

Likewise, we have done a thorough explanation of what salvation is; so, the purpose of this chapter is to gain a more vivid understanding of what true salvation is by examining what salvation is *not*.

What Salvation is Not

The physical act of uttering words in prayer form
In Hebrews 4 we read, "The Word of God had no effect because it was not coupled with faith." Isn't that a sobering statement—the fact that the truth of God landed on ears and it had no effect because it wasn't coupled with the heart of faith? If you show a man a cue card and he spouts off, "I admit that I'm a sinner. I believe in my heart. I commit and accept Jesus Christ," I cannot then say to him, "You're saved!" No, obviously not. Just getting someone to utter the words is not salvation. The prayer of salvation must come from a heart that understands lostness, or as my friend Alvin Reid says, "their emptiness." They must truly understand they are lost before they can know how to be saved and know the value of it. You should be very cautious and patient when getting someone to utter a prayer of salvation because their heart must already know it and believe it. I am sad to say that I can recall a time in my high school days that I went to New York City in an evangelistic outreach and, at a park bench, I was talking to a man. I had been hearing about people who had great experiences leading people to Christ and was hungry desiring to do the same because I didn't have a great story of leading someone to Christ as many others had experienced. So I determined in my heart that I would lead a person to the Lord and I remember sitting on that bench when a gentleman approached. I can even picture his face. I remember trying to rush him to the point to say "the prayer," and I remember telling him, "Just pray this and mean it in your heart." And I'd pray it, but he'd interrupt me and say, "But you know, I don't know." And I'd answer real quickly, "Just say this prayer." And I remember he got through the whole prayer and I thought to myself, "I feel so bad because I just ushered him into the act of simply uttering words."

He walked away; I never saw him again and probably never will. I pray to God that He grips that man's heart and doesn't allow that scenario to skew his thinking and mind about the Gospel. You see salvation is so much more than words. In fact, if an individual hears and recognizes the truth of the Gospel and the state of their lostness, you can then explain to them how they can have an intimate relationship with God. You can explain the truth of Jesus Christ and how He is the God who came to earth, died for us and defeated death through His resurrection. You can share how the person needs to believe these cognitive facts but also volitionally trust Christ. The prayer, I believe, is more of a confirmation or an affirmation for you, the mature believer, to listen in to see if they understood what they did, but frankly they could be saved before they ever utter that prayer. It's the heart that trusts; the mind that cognitively knows, but the heart that trusts. In Romans 10:9-10 we read, "If you confess with your mouth the Lord Jesus and believe in your heart that God has raised Him from the dead then you will be saved." In the Jewish tradition, you could not say you were a believer without coupling it with action. It was absolutely, unequivocally, positively impossible to say "I'm a believer" and not live it in the 1st century Jewish custom. In Acts, when Paul says, "Repent and be baptized," we see that repentance is what literally brings salvation. The words expressing our faith in Christ are simply a confirmation of what has occurred inside us.

The physical act of walking down an aisle in a church during an invitation

Again, when people believe on Jesus Christ in their hearts during a church service, they are saved before they ever walk down the aisle. And maybe the prayer at the altar is confirming to us as believers who prayerfully watch as people come to Christ. As long as people cognitively believe and their heart is stirred to salvation, they are probably saved prior to that physical act of walking down the aisle.

Contingent on a great emotion (or the lack of) during the conversion experience

Some individuals, when they're leading a person to Christ, will gauge the success or effectiveness of this endeavor on the emotional reaction of that individual. This is not a good gauge at all. Emotion is based on personality and is no indication of spirituality or whether or not salvation "took." Some cry, and some laugh. I remember leading a man to the altar, explaining the truths of Christ and praying with him as He received salvation. After praying at the altar he stood up, shook my hand and simply said, "That was the right thing to do. That was good that I did that." No tears. Conversely, some people who accept Christ do so and are just bawling and raising their hands and dancing all around. The way in which emotion will be expressed will be reflected in the personalities of individuals. Just like worship services, the spirit may work mightily and the congregation could be dead quiet. If it's filled with a room full

22

of introverts then they're going to be very introspective when they get moved by the truths of the song and Scripture, and they're going to maybe even bow their heads and pray. You cannot gauge even your own worship on emotion and outward expression; it must be the heart stirring and it may not always be an overt expression.

The result of solely wanting to be saved from going to hell upon death
"Do you want to go to heaven or hell?" I am always curious if the person who asks this question expects to receive a different answer than "Heaven" from the person who is asked the question. Therefore, I don't know if this is a good question to ask as it may skew and ignore the full teaching of salvation that we have been discussing in this chapter. As a parent, I can't help but liken it to the question some parents often ask their child, "Do you want a spanking?" Think about what the child is going to say. Have we ever heard a child respond, "Yes! Actually, I'd like a double dose?" Who would not choose heaven?

Here's the problem, people don't understand the value of salvation until they understand their lostness. They don't understand the value of being saved without first knowing that they are lost. But suffice it to say that because of our sinful state we have merited or earned condemnation to hell. It's not God being mean to us; we've done it to ourselves. When a student of mine fails a course, I will say, "I did not fail you. You failed yourself by what you did or didn't do and you are reaping the consequences of your actions." Likewise, because of our sinful state — because I'm not perfect, like God and I'm not as holy as He is — there is no way I am worthy of heaven without God in me. I'm not holy and my sinful heart that is repulsive to God condemns me. I deserve eternal punishment for my sinful state. Therefore, I (and all sinners) need a change of heart that is life-changing and soul-changing. We need salvation through Christ.

The topic of hell should never be avoided because it is the inevitable outcome for those who do not accept Christ after they hear they are not at peace with God, hear they are in close relationship with God's wrath (Ephesians 2:3), and do not accept Christ's payment to appease the Father's wrath. But hear me, I personally am of the conviction that if I turn to someone and ask, "Do you want to go to heaven or hell," they may not at that point fully understand their emptiness, and the fact that they are the enemy of God. So I suggest that hell should definitely be part of the salvation equation, but people who pray for salvation may not be thinking at the time, "I am not going to be punished eternally." The reason we are not saved is because we are not at peace with the Holy God, our Creator. As I said earlier, our Creator is the Holy One, and we must commit our lives to Him and ask forgiveness for how we have separated ourselves from Him and created the gulf between us through our sin. And hell is a byproduct of the repercussion for not believing.

Translated into instant perfection

As stated in the previous chapter, the Bible disperses the full teaching of a particular doctrine within a number of related verses. But there are three terms that can summarize the different aspects of the salvation process.

Occasionally when the Scriptures use and refer to the word *saved* or salvation, it is actually used ina few different ways. It is used sometimes amorally; like you're saved from a ship sinking or you're saved from a crowd wanting to stone this individual, literally just protection. The word *salvation* was not a spiritual term that biblical writers made up, it was a very practical term that was adopted to explain the saving of our souls. Hence, the word *saved* has taken on this real spiritual meaning and it has great depth. So when we read Scripture sometimes when it uses the word saved it means the point in which you were justified, sanctified, or glorified. Let me explain.

Justification – Saved from the penalty of sin
The moment an individual is saved from the penalty of sin, we literally move from darkness to light, change course from hell to heaven, and gain peace with God. Sometimes the Bible uses the words *saved* or *salvation* to refer to the moment Christ redeems us. At the moment of salvation, the individual is sealed by the Holy Spirit and becomes a child of God—a Christian. This is called justification. In fact, in Romans, Paul uses this word to describe that moment—it is a judicial act or a declaration wherein God declares, "You are justified!" It's as if a judge slams down the gavel and authoritatively states, "Done deal!"

Sanctification – Saved from the power of sin
Sometimes in Scripture, the word saved is referring to our developmental growth, spiritual growth, or maturity. Philippians 2 says, "*Work out your own salvation*." This is not referring to the justification aspect of salvation because you can't work out your own salvation, but you can work for and develop and be in process of your spiritual maturity. And that's exactly what some of the terms for salvation refers to -- sanctification. Once we are saved we are to be utilizing the power of the Holy Spirit against the power of sin. The more you are sanctified, the more you are maturing, the more power you have against sinning because the power source of the Holy Spirit within you. You have a mind that has been inculcated by His truths. You are to be constantly storing away and hiding God's Word in your heart. It is a "lamp unto your feet, a light unto your path," and you are maturing and now you have the ability by God's power alone to say, "I'm not going to go down those old paths of sin again."

Before our salvation, according to Ephesians 2:1-3, we could not say no to sin. We could say, "I don't like doing these things," but we had no power to overcome the grip of sin. We, as sinners, were encased by sin. There was no way to jump out of that realm into the realm of the Holy Spirit. Now that we're in the saved realm, the Holy Spirit allows us to confidently state, "I don't want to do that action." We've been saved from the penalty of sin and we gain an immediate power source that is our strength to overcoming the sins that once plagued our lives. We can be controlled by the Spirit (Ephesians 5:18) and therefore do not have to give into the desires of our flesh.

Glorification – Saved from the presence of sin
Sometimes the word *salvation* will refer to the consummation of our salvation. In fact, Scripture writers will use the word *saved* to refer to our future salvation. The fact that the "helmet of salvation" (Ephesians 6:10-17) is looking at the future aspect of salvation means that one day we, as Christians, will be saved from this world and from this environment of sin. As Christians, our salvation is settled—a done deal. But one day we will be saved from the presence of sin when we see God face to face. There will be no more warring of the soul (Romans 7) and sin won't even be a variable in our lives. That's a beautiful place! To think that someday we won't have this battle within us. We will be in the presence of the Holy One.

Recently, I was lecturing on the benefits of heaven. I noted that we will be able to think and remember, worship, learn, work and enjoy it. You and I will be on the other side and we'll say, "Hey let's go worship the Holy One for a millennia or two!" And we'll just zip into His presence. We'll also recognize people and be able to talk to them, and know who our loved ones are by name. What a beautiful place! There will be no sun because the glory of God illuminates the sky. Titus 2:11-13 tells us, "*For the grace of God that brings salvation has appeared to all men* (Justification), *teaching us that denying ungodliness and worldly lust, we should live soberly, righteously and godly in this present world* (sanctification), *looking for that blessed hope and the glorious appearing of our great God and Savior Jesus Christ*" (glorification). All three of these salvific terms are found in that one passage. These terms are important to know because we evangelize to bring someone to God in order to be justified. We see that there is an accountability, or a discipleship process, that we must be involved in all the way through to glorification— it never ends. Salvation is a glorious promise and a wonderful gift of God.

Am I Saved?

Now that we have taken some time to learn about what salvation is and what salvation is not, I want you to ask yourself the most important question that you will ever be asked. Ask yourself, "*Am I Saved?*"

We have covered a lot of ground in terms of the salvation experience and our desperate need for God because of our sin. But I want to ask you now if you are indeed a child of God. You may have been in church for a long time and heard many of these principles articulated in the pulpit. But as I've noted, salvation is more than simply hearing the message. If you examine your life, can you remember a time that you knelt before God and said, "I am a sinner and I need You to save me." Maybe there has never been a time that you processed these things and cognitively looked at what you needed to know and believe in your heart to be saved. You didn't quite comprehend your lostness and haven't committed your heart and trusted Christ solely for salvation. I don't know where you are spiritually. Maybe you've lived in a Christian home and have possibly lived off your parents' belief. There's never been a time where you have processed these things until now and you ask yourself, "Do I acknowledge this? Do I cognitively know this? Do I believe this in my heart? Have I volitionally, of my own will, committed and trusted? Am I totally dependent on Him?"

Be cautioned. You can be right in the middle of the church house and be lost! You can be like Judas Iscariot who walked with God for over three years and was lost. You can be like the Apostle Paul who, prior to his salvation experience, knew the Scripture writings but was looking at it through carnal eyes - as a works-based faith. He was essentially saying, "What can I do to get saved?" When he actually got saved, he was able to immediately become a strong minister because he knew all the truth from before but was able to now look at it through spiritual eyes—Christ's eyes. You may know the scriptures and all the spiritual words that so many Christians utter, but you may have learned after reading this chapter that you need to look at it differently now.

The question is this: If right now, you are not sure that you're saved, as defined in this chapter based on God's Holy Word, would you like to take care of it right now – this moment? Would you bow your head and get in whatever posture that would cause you to focus on Him and ask God to forgive you and save you today?

What Must I Do?

In your heart you must (1) believe that He is God; that He visited this earth and lived a sinless and pure life, died on the cross to make payment for your sin, arose from the tomb and invites everyone to believe in Him; (2) believe that He arose the third day to give unequivocal proof that He is sufficient to conquer death and He will conquer the spiritual death in our lives; (3) believe your soul will be eternally His if you know those facts and couple it with a heart of faith and put your dependence and trust in Him; and (4) commit these things to Him by saying, "I believe You and I will entrust my whole life based on this truth. My foundation will now be grounded on the truths of Jesus Christ, the Holy One of God."

Finally, in your own way, ask Him to be your Savior. And then, simply just thank Him for saving you and thank Him that He has opened your eyes to your need of salvation.

If you have done this, God has washed and cleansed you, and your soul is as white as snow! God will give you a power source to say no to your temptation and to live for Him. You are beginning today as a Christian, as a child of God!

If you accepted Christ just now, I pray that you will inform someone of your decision or contact me directly at Liberty University and I would love to rejoice with you. You also should get involved in a church that will teach the principles of this lecture from God's Word and that you will stick to these fundamentals.

Write It Down

Do any of the points explaining what salvation is not apply to your life? Did any one point personally surprise you, or cause you to think about what salvation is no? If so, write down your experience...

_____

_____

_____

_____

_____

_____

_____

_____

_____

_____

_____

Take some time to think about your salvation experience (if applicable). How do you know for certain that you are saved? If you are not, what has this chapter caused your mind and heart to ponder?

_____

_____

_____

_____

_____

_____

_____

_____

_____

_____

_____

_____

_____

_____

_____

_____

_____

_____

_____

Notes

Walk

CHAPTER THREE

Walk Close

I had always heard that children born just a couple years apart can be totally opposite in personality. After the Lord blessed us with two daughters, I have found that to indeed be true. Both of my daughters are beautiful, kind, and caring. I love their unique personalities and adore them both equally. But there is a distinct difference on how each of them expresses their love and desires to receive expressions of love.

My oldest daughter desires hugs, kisses, and words of affirmation. My youngest daughter spells love "T-I-M-E"! Of course, she appreciates hugs, kisses, and words of affirmation, but will willingly cut the hug-time short in lieu of grabbing something for both of us to play with together. Regardless of how different their personalities are, my love for them is the same!

When either one of my daughters come up to me in their own unique way, my words to them are always the same. In fact, by now, they can predict exactly what is the first thing I will tell them. They are prepared for me to say, "I love you more than you can EVER imagine! Do you know that I love you?" To which they reply, "yep, Dad." Then I say, "*NO*, do you really know how much I love you?" To which they reply with a slight giggle as they are now anticipating my unannounced tickle spell, "Yes, Dad!" "Yes, Dad, What?" I say. "Yes, Dad, I know you love me!" Then it is an all-out tickle fest as I try to dig in and they try feverously to wiggle away.

After we calm down a little I always let them know, "I am so proud of you!" Not because of what they have done for me, or the fun they have allowed me to have with them, but because of who they are and our strong bond of intimacy and appreciation for each other. It is the same with our relationship in Jesus Christ.

There is one question we must regularly ask ourselves as we move forward through a life with Christ – "God, Are You Pleased With Me?" Whether you are a student, a Bible teacher, a pastor, or even a lay-worker, it is important to silently reflect on this question often, as I believe it searches the deepest parts of who we are and our intimacy with God.

Luke 15 examines the value of a relationship with God, and through three specific parables, the author describes very familiar cultural themes that underline two key elements of the Christian life – evangelism and discipleship. I believe we need to look at these three parables together and avoid the common mistake of considering them individually. These parables speak of sheep and shepherds, a woman who possesses money, and a father and his two sons. Luke 15 is written for us to read intently, experiencing the story as it unfolds. As we read, we need to imagine shaking the dust off our sandals with the shepherds, feeling the panic of losing a valuable coin, and hearing the painful words of a boy to his father. Experiencing the text will help us understand the importance of our relationship with our heavenly Father, and it helps us to see that He sought us, found us, and rejoices in our acceptance of Him.

An Evangelistic Emphasis

In these three biblical parables, we can see three words: *seek, find,* and *rejoice.* Let's look at verse four, the Parable of the Lost Sheep:

"What man among you, if he has a hundred sheep and has lost one of them, does not leave the ninety-nine in the open pasture and go after the one which is lost until he finds it?" (Luke 15:4)

In verse five, we see that the shepherd does find his lost sheep, and in verse seven, a correlation is drawn between the sheep returning to the flock and a man/woman coming to God:

"I tell you that in the same way, there will be more joy (or rejoicing) in heaving (heaven) over one sinner who repents than over ninety-nine righteous persons who need no repentance." (Luke 15:7)

This shepherd has lost one of his sheep, but then he discovers it and brings it back to the fold. And what does he do next? He has a party, calling all of his friends and neighbors (vs. 6) to rejoice with Him. He sought the sheep, he found the sheep, and then he rejoiced at the sheep's return. *Seek. Find. Rejoice.*

In the Parable of the Lost Son, we see a father with two sons, but one has gone astray, and the father is looking for the son to return home. When the wayward son finally returns, the father throws a huge party saying, "'For this son of mine was dead and has come to life again; he was lost and has been found.' And they began to celebrate." Once again, we see this important evangelistic principle that should undergird all of our witnessing efforts – *Seek. Find. Rejoice.*

A Christian Life Emphasis

I can't think of a better passage to talk about in terms of evangelism and the Christian life than Luke 15 because we're talking about; (1) exerting the effort to go out; (2) the joy of finding a person in need of the Savior, and (3) rejoicing together when a lost soul repents and comes to Christ. But we also must not forget to employ the discipleship or spiritual component of these three parables because there are some brilliant spiritual truths here that can help us understand our relationship with God with new insight.

Jesus addressed non-believers first

In this chapter in Luke, we see how God's Word applies to all. There are a lot of people in the crowd Jesus is addressing as He teaches through the use of these three parables. Jesus is actually attempting a very daunting task; having to convey a salvation message to thousands of people, with myriads of backgrounds, lifestyles, and social statuses. He had to have the same words splinter out, and have unique application to everybody.

Two particular groups are the Pharisees and the scribes (Luke 15:2), and they listen as Jesus begins to speak. Even though they are listening, they are not interested in His words, rather more interested in condemning Him; noting that Jesus has been eating with publicans and sinners. It is clear Jesus had a diverse audience, and I believe these holier-than-thou scribes and Pharisees shut their ears to His words, compelling Jesus to direct his teachings to believers.

I don't think Jesus completely divorced His conversation from non-believers, in fact I'm sure some continued to listen in throughout, but seemingly not the hard-nosed Pharisees and scribes who oddly enough were the ones who literally transcribed the Word of God. It appears these scholarly men literally became too educated, too smart, and too prejudiced to be able to understand the implications of Jesus' words. As written throughout the gospels, we see the Lord doing a masterful job of conveying truth to all individuals involved as he recounts these three parables.

Jesus addressed believers second

In the undercurrent of these parables, we also can see the tone of discipleship and evangelism – which is important to believers. We learn through these three parables the importance of a believer's relationship with his/her heavenly Father, and we see how God rewards our efforts of seeking, finding, and rejoicing over lost souls that have been saved. Let's take a further look at the truths found in these remarkable parables.

One Hundred to One

Luke 15:1-7

This is a dramatic and vivid parable about evangelism that is followed by an encouraging word to those in Christ. Jesus points to the heart of a shepherd who loves and values all of his sheep equally, but the Pharisees and scribes did not understand this concept. In fact, many scholars have suggested that the Pharisees would rather Jesus have phrased the parable this way:

"What man of you owning one hundred sheep, having a hired hand to tend over the sheep, doesn't receive a report from his hired hand and command the hired hand to run out and find a sheep when it is lost?"

The Pharisees lacked humility. They were puffed up with their own importance and couldn't see themselves performing the tasks of a shepherd. Instead, they needed humility and a proper view of self because the wisdom of this parable did not resonate in their minds at all. Before teaching a spiritual principle, Jesus first tells these men that they need to humble themselves in the sight of the Lord, and realize – as we also see in Matthew 5 – that they (and we) need to be poor in spirit. Naturally, they were too lofty to understand this and thought much too highly of themselves to change.

Not only does Jesus expound upon the importance of humility, but He also describes some profound principles for those who are in Christ. In verse five, we see that after the shepherd has found the lost sheep, he lovingly places it on his shoulders and carries it back to the fold. Let's take a look at the reasons why that sheep might have been lost.

First, the sheep probably did not consciously or purposely leave the flock. It somehow veered off course and got separated from the rest. There is no doubt it was scared to be alone, and then it heard the shepherd's familiar and comforting voice calling for it. Another possible reason is that it might have been so sick that its ears were infected and it couldn't hear (or recognize) the shepherd's voice. Just as when we are spiritually sick, we cannot recognize the voice of our Shepherd when He is calling us to return to Him. I'm reminded of John 10, "My sheep hear my voice, I know them and they follow me." The third likely reason is that the sheep was simply rebellious. He might have heard the shepherd's voice earlier and he simply ran away. No matter why the sheep was lost – through accident, sickness, or rebellion – the shepherd lifted it up on his shoulders and carried it home.

An important point to note is that if a sheep was rebellious, it was a common practice among shepherds at this time to break one of the sheep's leg before he put it on his shoulders to carry it back to the flock. The sheep would literally be unable to walk for several weeks, meaning that everywhere the herd traveled, the shepherd would have to carry it on his shoulders. During this time, the sheep would hear the shepherd's voice, smell his scent, and feel his touch. When the sheep reached full recovery, it would remain very near to the shepherd at all times, maybe even tripping him up from time to time, because the sheep had experienced the comfort of being near it's master.

In Psalm 51 David prayed, "Create in me a clean heart . . . so that the bones which thou hast broken may rejoice." David, in his confession of sin through adultery with Bathsheba, remembered his days as a shepherd and is probably recalling here the times he had to break a rebellious sheep's leg and how it related related to his own brokenness.

It's Personal
This picture of a shepherd carrying his sheep describes how God's compassion is great and how personal His commitment is to us. We see that He would ideally leave others behind so that He can individually tend to our condition specifically. It's a sobering realization to see that we are of great interest to Him and He will seek to find us when we are lost, spiritually sick, or even rebellious. God is most definitely interested in your personal situation!

A True Friend
Sometimes a real friend has to practice what we call "tough love." This means that they love us to the point of risking the friendship in order to point out something in our life that we cannot see for ourselves. Isn't that a true friend? One who is willing to say the tough things to us? Sure, it's difficult to take sometimes; it's never easy to hear how you are disappointing or hurting your friend(s), but eventually if you are honest with yourself you come to see that your friend's words are true and necessary.

Likewise, sometimes God needs to figuratively break our leg so that we will realize the necessity of being close to Him, allowing Him to provide special ministry to us. In that moment we are being picked up while the ninety-nine that don't need repentance carry on in the field. This parable is a picture of God's tough love at times, and His ultimate promise to protect us – His rebellious children.

Luke 15:8-10
In verses 8-10, Jesus tells the Parable of the Lost Coin. The learned men again close off their ears; they don't want to hear a story about a *woman*! Unfortunately, in the 1st Century, a woman was not seen as capable of teaching anybody – especially a man. In fact, it was odd for a woman to sit at the feet of a rabbi. That is why in Luke 10:38, where we see Mary sitting at the feet of Jesus, the disciples saw this as strange. Remember the Samaritan woman in John 4? After having an encounter with Jesus at the well, she rushed back to her city saying, "Come see a man that has told me everything I was!" And then she asks, "Is this not the Christ?" In the Greek text this passage is phrased this way, "Come see a man that has told me all that I ever was, but this isn't the Christ, is it?" It wasn't that she didn't know that she had been speaking with the Christ; it was a cultural issue. She knew men wouldn't listen to her, and so she played to their cultural ignorance. And so she adds, "We'll see for ourselves." Later, after people in the city believed, they said, "Now we believe, not because of her saying, but because we have seen with our eyes."

One of my colleagues describes Luke's Gospel as "The Great Reversal." If you notice, Luke uses a lot of individuals who are lowly in status to make great spiritual points. To have a shepherd or a woman be the focus of a great spiritual truth is unusual, or as my colleague would say, it's "the great reversal." Society saw these individuals as having no status at all, but the Lord lifts them up. The parable of the Good Samaritan, also in this Gospel, is similar. For Jewish people to learn from a Samaritan was unthinkable – the great reversal. So, we see Jesus was again going to teach them that humility is needed in their lives, and they desperately need a proper view of self, but their pride will be the end of them.

Maintaining a Positive Spiritual Testimony
In the Parable of the Lost Coin, a woman has ten coins and loses one. In the 1st Century, to sweep a home was virtually impossible because the floor was often parched dirt. This woman most likely would have had little to no light, having to use a candle to see between the crevices and cracks. She might have literally searched for days. Why would a woman go to all that trouble for just one coin? And why, after she found it, would she actually throw a party? Seems rather strange to us, but yet again the cultural context is profound.

Scholars are quick to point out that in culture women who were engaged would often wear ten coins in a garland around their head, signifying they were engaged. To lose one of these coins was like losing an engagement ring. So now we understand why this woman was painstakingly searching for her lost coin. If she didn't find it, people might think she had a blatant disregard for her groom, and she saw her relationship with him as careless and unimportant. This is why we see her rejoicing in such an outspoken manner, joyous at finding the lost coin.

Here is the significance of this story to believers. We must be concerned with our appearance when non-believers look at us; we must be concerned with how we are presenting ourselves as followers of Christ. We cannot appear to have a careless relationship with our Savior – as this woman would have appeared if she had lost one of her ten valued coins. Simply put, our deeds must back up our words. James tells us that faith without works is absolutely meaningless, even dead.

Early on in my marriage, I got careless with where I put my wedding ring. In fact, I put it in my backpack during a softball game – so I thought. When I returned home, I couldn't find it and I had to tell her that I'd lost it. She was naturally hurt that I would be so careless with the ring; it was a symbol of our marriage. Nothing I said seemed to console her. Finally, I found the ring a few days later in a backpack, and after that experience, I realized even more the importance of the symbol of my love for my wife.

We must always protect the symbols of our devotion to Christ. We cannot be careless in how we present ourselves to the public. This passage tells us that we must, (1) be concerned with our spiritual testimony and constantly examine our lives to see if things we are doing might hinder someone coming to Christ, (2) never allow the liberties we have as New Testament Christians to get to the point where we say, "I'm going to do what I want and others will just have to get over it," and (3) we must strive to maintain integrity. We see that this woman searched *diligently* for the lost coin because it was a symbol of her testimony – her commitment to her fiancé.

I see all of the time, those who are in Christ belittling their testimony. They do not value their testimony the way they should. They are careless. All of us must remember this woman and the shepherd, and how their stories relate to us.

Two Sons

Luke 15:11-32

It's a story of a father and his two sons. Now, unlike the first two stories, I'm certain Jesus got the attention of the Pharisees with this parable. They could relate to what Christ was saying in verse 11, "a certain man had two sons . . . and this son says to his father, 'Give me my inheritance.'" Here's why this verse is so strange. An inheritance was given to a son only upon the death of the father. This young man was essentially saying, "I wish you were dead because I just want the money that is coming to me." The Pharisees, who I'm sure have sons, are intrigued by this story. Those in the crowd who do not believe, are most likely starting to feel the sting of this young man's statement. Once again, Jesus addresses the importance of humility and the proper view of self.

Verse 13 says it wasn't long after the son received his inheritance that he was involved in "foolish living." The word used denotes that he was "scattered" as in Matthew 13, "you sow seeds, you scatter the seeds." Verse 14 tells us that he had soon "spent all there was," and he was reduced to taking a job feeding pigs – a Jewish boy was feeding unclean (not Kosher) animals. He had been reduced to doing the unthinkable – things he would have never done when he was in the good graces of his father. What a profound truth to think on regarding sin. If sin in our life is not addressed, we can fall into a place we once never thought we were capable of falling. In verse 16, we see that it got even worse; he ate the husk and garbage that the pigs ate!

In verse 17, we read that after reaching the very depth of a life entangled in wrong living, the son finally "came to himself." It's the very thing Jesus was hoping the Pharisees would do when they heard this story. The audience sees in this young man a transfer from pride to humility, as the son realizes his need to return home amid his defeat. Finally, after the son "came to himself," we see that there was great rejoicing. The father, after waiting and watching for his son, shouts, "My son is alive again – he was lost, now he is found!" And the party began.

Come Home

There are valuable lessons for all within this story. For those in Christ, God desires to have fellowship with us – no matter where we have gone to escape Him (like the rebellious sheep and the prodigal son). As he did with Paul, God calls us. He wants to have fellowship with His children, He always forgives, and He welcomes home those who have gone astray. On the other hand, this story shows us that God takes interest in all, even those who don't believe.

It's important to see that often times our words have a strong influence on those who have gone astray. There are seasons in your life when words are of the utmost effectiveness.. We will be able to reason with those we love, cite Scripture to touch their hearts, and watch their hearts return to their relationship with Jesus. Conersly, there will be times when your words can be counterproductive. Do you think that this young man would have listened to words of warning about his behavior before his money ran out or before he fell into total despair? Certainly not – the words would have been wasted. The Lord says that after words have played out their season, we should be quiet and revert to deep prayer. The father of the son understood this. He loved his son and wanted him home, but he knew that chasing him down would do no good. He had to let his son's rebellion run its course, and so he remained in prayer, ready for the day he could welcome him home.

Situations like this enhance our faith and certainly our prayer life. In our desperation, as our words fall on the deaf ears of a friend or loved one, we call out to God. I sometimes wish God would choose a different type of lesson to teach us to trust Him, but he knows these seasons of heartache will teach us to trust Him unlike any other. When you are burdened for the soul of a non-believer or a believer who has fallen into the pigpen of life because of his or her rebelliousness, fall to your knees and cultivate your spiritual relationship with God. This will strengthen you more than you know. Further, don't be like the brother who, upon his brother's return complained, "Hey, I've been the faithful one here and now my brother is getting all the attention!" We need to have hearts like the father (and our Holy Father); always ready to celebrate with those who come home – even those who have done us wrong.

Regaining Intimacy with God

Elements of True Confession

Let's take a look at Psalm 51 and the context of this great passage about confession. It's a psalm from the heart of David, who is asking God to restore him to the fellowship and intimacy he once had with God - and that he so greatly misses. Have you ever known someone who was living for Christ but, for some reason, they fell away? It is certainly troubling when this occurs. David fell away because of the adulterous affair with Bathsheba that I mentioned earlier. In this psalm, he is confessing not just his sin, but also the sin of plotting the murder of her husband, who also happened to be a dear friend of his. "Have mercy upon me oh God!" David cries out. He is in pain because of his sin – his testimony has been shot. He cannot be an effective king or representative of God, all because he has become spiritually corrupt. He longs to return to spiritual purity, wanting to be like one of the sheep that he cared for as a boy.

David is acknowledging his mistake, and admits, "It is always before me." His sin haunts him. Have you ever been there? Now, you may not think your sin is as gross as David's, but that may be an indication of apathy in your heart (I'm living alright and I'm not doing many bad things). This spirit of apathy is often more difficult and challenging to deal with than it is with someone who is overtly fallen into sin. Often times, when we know "the script," we tend to fall into complacency about our behavior. This is a dangerous place to be because we don't see a need for repentance, and we don't realize that we are not living in harmony with Christ.

How do you get away from that place of spiritual lethargy? How do you restore the incredible intimacy you once had with Christ? You may have to go all the way back to your salvation experience in order to remember how you fell in love with God, and how you were touched by the things of Christ. Your early days of salvation can be your point of reference to regain intimacy with the Father. In 1 Peter 2:2, we see that we are "living stones." This refers to Joshua 4, where people would put up stones as memorials so that everyone who walked by them would recall the mighty things that God did for them. Maybe you need to go back and find an old symbol of your early and heartfelt faith – an old Bible, a devotional book, photos of you with those who were most influential in your life. Those symbols can serve as a "living stone" so that we can recall – and others can see in us – what God has done in and through us.

I remind you once more of the importance of seeing these three parables collectively rather than individually. Jesus had to address the crowd three separate times, but had the same message to all. He emphasizes the importance of humility, but he also expounded upon a transformed life impacted by three simple truths. *Seek. Find. Rejoice.*

write It Down

Take a few minutes to site in silence, and after reflecting, ask God if He is pleased with you. What was spoken to your heart?

_____

_____

_____

_____

_____

_____

_____

_____

_____

_____

What do the three simple truths — Seek, Find, and Rejoice mean to you in light of how they are discussed in this chapter?

_____

_____

_____

_____

_____

_____

_____

_____

_____

_____

_____

_____

_____

_____

_____

_____

_____

_____

Notes

CHAPTER FOUR

Walk Guarded

I'm a roller coaster freak!! I absolutely love roller coasters. In Williamsburg, VA at Busch Gardens, there is this ride called The Griffon and it is amazing. You get on, there are three rows, and if you have sandals on you have to kick them off, because there's no ground. It's really cruel, what the Griffon does, because it takes you around very slow at first. It takes you up 240 feet, and instead of instantaneously dropping you; they let you enjoy the scenery for a while. They take you around a horseshoe – and then they start you up what is the nastiest hill you've ever seen. That's when prayer time begins! You don't pray for God's blessings in life, you pray for the basic necessities of life! "God, I just want to feel concrete under my feet when this is all over!" This hill is 90-degrees straight down, and they don't just whip you down quickly, they suspend you in mid air, hanging there, allowing you to contemplate your fate. It's during these times I think, "Why am I on this *thing*!" What seems like forever, suddenly you hear the worst sound that chills you – "click." Why is it that freaks like me get back in line? I can't get enough! After about the fifth time, while suspending in the air, I thought of Ephesians 4. Sounds crazy, I know, but it makes sense.

Sin starts out slow, but before you know it, the rush of it is surrounding you. You find yourself going back for more and more, and soon you find yourself in a spiritual condition virtually impossible to escape.

Ephesians 4:17-19 – A Six-Step Digression
We see that in the spiritual realm it is a wise man or woman who says, "Search me oh God and know my heart..." (Psalm 139). We must always have our hearts open to God and welcome His presence in our hearts and minds. In this chapter, I'd like to ask you to put yourself under the scrutiny of God's Word, and be honest enough to ask God to give you a spiritual spanking, if that is what is needed in your life. We all need one of those—just like a child needs discipline from his or her parents every now and then, because we learn from the experience.

The question "How did I get spiritually sick?" is one that some people may never ask of themselves. I think many people might fear such a question, or they may fear the answer. We sometimes think of ourselves as incapable of becoming spiritually sick, but we can all reach this state. I pray that the spiritual conditioning and mentoring that I am prescribing in this chapter is effective in helping you avoid spiritual sickness. Further, I want to say that there is no shame in admitting that there are seasons when you need to be refreshed. I need such seasons myself. If you are not spiritually strong right now, there is no shame in taking a sabbatical—a time when you say, "I must be spiritually filled."

A student approached me some time ago and said, "I have asked eight Christian leaders who are very influential people in my life, if I should step down from my youth pastorate position." The problem was that this young man, who was a student as well as a local youth pastor, was in a promiscuous relationship with his girlfriend, whom he planned to marry. My first question to him was: "What did these godly men/women say to you?" He told me that all eight had instructed him that he could remain in his position if he committed to work on this sin—every single one of them! And I leaned back in my office chair and said, "What was their rationale for such a conclusion? How did they justify this advice they gave you?" He said that his pastor's statement to him could sum up the thinking. The pastor had told him: "You are still a student who is learning and your actions can be dismissed because of your youth." My heart grieved because this probably well-intentioned pastor, and others, had not told this young man to flee from his youthful lust. Instead, they suggested that he should simply "work on" steering clear of his lust and they essentially excused the fact that he was involved in a sinful lifestyle. I believe their words to him were wrong and dangerous.

You see, the Apostle Paul says we are to run away from sin; we are not to process our lust or allow it to make progress within us. In 1 Timothy 3, Paul lists the qualifications of bishops (or church leaders) and we must insist that our leaders meet these conditions of leadership. We cannot simply say to leaders who are involved in sin, "Just try to do better." Further, I believe the pastor and others who counseled this young man diminished his influence with his fellow students.

Let's examine Matthew 10:1 where Jesus did two things for the disciples, (1) He taught them, and (2) He empowered them to accomplish great things for Him. We see here that we are to become disciples and then apostles. He called them to learn and do. I think we sometimes underestimate the influence a student has with his peers. And so I told the student who came to me that I could not advise him to remain in his youth ministry position for a time. I could not put my stamp of approval on the service of a young man who was involved in the very sin that afflicts so many young people today. I encouraged him to take a rest from service, a sabbatical of sorts, so that he could seek wise counsel and spend time with God to seek forgiveness and empowerment to overcome his problem. "You need to step out of your role of leadership and get spiritually revived and purified again," I told him. And he asked me, "What will people say?" Knowing that the pastor had given him unwise counsel earlier, so I said, "Unfortunately, the pastor you are going to ask for this time off is one of the people who didn't see a need for you to step down. So I am going to pray that the Lord will give everyone involved in this situation the wisdom to handle this situation properly." And the most amazing thing happened. The young man went to his pastor and explained that he needed time away from his post in order to be spiritually revived, and the pastor replied in a remarkable way. He said, "You know, we have never done anything like this in our church, but I think this is wise. I think it will teach and mentor a lot of people." And the pastor prayed with the young man, asking that God would bless in his time of renewal.

The next Wednesday night, the young man explained to his youth group his need for spiritual renewal and another amazing thing happened. After the meeting, several young people, including the leaders, told this young man that they too were spiritually dry. They thanked him for admitting his weakness and his spiritual need of renewal and began to consider their own spiritual needs.

You see, God will work in our lives when we cast our cares and burdens on Him. He wants us to come to Him with our problems and our weaknesses. He wants us to lean on Him as a child leans on his father. Here's the best part of the story; I can testify to you today that this young man is back in the same ministry and he is engaged to be married to the young lady and, best of all, he's a spiritually strong minister for the body of Christ. There is no shame in asking the serious spiritual question, "Am I spiritually sick?" And there is no dishonor in stepping out of leadership for a time of spiritual renewal when we determine that we have indeed become spiritually sick.

Today I want to take you through a portion of Scripture that describes how we can become spiritually sick, or dry inside. Let's look at Ephesians 4:17-19, a detailed portion of Scripture in the middle of Paul's letter to the Ephesians. We read, "*This I say, therefore, and testify in the Lord, that you should no longer walk as the rest of the Gentiles walk, in the futility of their mind, having their understanding darkened, being alienated from the life of God, because of the ignorance that is in them, because of the blindness of their heart, who, being past feeling, have given themselves over to lewdness, to work all uncleanness with greediness.*"

Herein, we see a six-step digression or a path that every person walks down when they're on the way to becoming spiritually sick. Unfortunately, most people on this course typically do not recognize that they're heading down this path until the third, fourth or fifth step. Let's examine what these steps are in Ephesians 4:17-19.

> **STEP 1:** Futility of their mind
> **STEP 2:** Darkened understanding
> **STEP 3:** Blindness of the heart
> **STEP 4:** Past feeling
> **STEP 5:** Lewdness
> **STEP 6:** Greediness

A couple of times, I have had the difficult task of being in a position of confronting men who have fallen into adultery. It is a very sobering thing to look a man in the eyes and say, "You have been named in having an adulterous affair." As the sin has been exposed, I've seen men try to find a way out or act like a cornered, wounded animal. While the reactions were somewhat varied, each man essentially said the same tragic thing; "I never thought this would happen to me. I never thought I would be in a position like this." Listen, this six-step digression is something that can happen to any of us if we do not remain in tune with and controlled by the Holy Spirit. We must always meditate on the truths of the Holy Spirit.

I want to examine this six-step digression step-by-step so that we can later learn how to avoid these pitfalls we create for ourselves.

Futility of The Mind

Some Bible versions use the term "the vanity of the mind." When this occurs, we are essentially saying: "I know the Bible harps on what I'm doing and that it is frowned upon, but I'm not sure it is really wrong." We start using all sorts of counseling words to mask the fact that we are involved in sin. People in this situation often say: "I'm not really hurting anyone." Their mind rationalizes their sin. I've seen Christians try to justify just about every type of sin. Proverbs 3:5-6 tells us: "Trust in the Lord with all your heart, and lean not on your own understanding; in all your ways acknowledge Him, and He shall direct your paths."

When we do not allow God to direct our path, we can get off on many strange and treacherous roads because we allow our own minds to trick us into thinking we are not doing anything wrong. People in this step typically are not involved in daily prayer, Bible reading, and intentional spiritual discussions with other believers. Subsequently, when we start to believe that we don't need to pray or read our Bibles as often as we once did, our actions will begin to reflect the vanity of our minds. And soon we will start rationalizing things through our own logic that in our spirit we know to be wrong. Sadly, many Christians never recognize this step because they have indeed blinded themselves to the futility of their own minds.

Darkened Understanding

Step 2 is what I call "the fuzzy step." People involved in Step 1 are often able to debate their action (sin) and they might even be able to do it somewhat effectively, even though they are wrong. But those who reach Step 2 must begin to debate what is better and best, which will ead to justifying what is patently wrong. Christians who reach this step are at a point where their minds do not have a default system that goes to God's Word for answers to questions regarding their life and behavior. In fact, the Word of God begins to become like a high-pitched noise to a dog, and these Christians begin to figuratively tilt their head from side to side as the strangeness of the Bible loses its resonance with them. What a terrible fate to bring on to oneself. These Christians should know better than to reach this point, but they have allowed their understanding to become darkened.

In turn, better and best decisions become fuzzy propositions. Philippians 1:9-10 states: "*And this I pray, that your love may abound still more and more in knowledge and all discernment, that you may approve the things that are excellent, that you may be sincere and without offense till the day of Christ.*" This is where we want to be. When we are discerning, we will literally have the spiritual shrewdness to test any issue without fear. We must all seek to have true spiritual discernment so that we never reach the place where better and best issues become fuzzy because we have allowed our minds, our understanding, to be darkened. When this happens, things, as we'll see in the next step, get progressively worse!

Blindness of The Heart

Have you ever traveled to Mammoth Cave in Kentucky? It's a wonderful place. While you're there, a guide will take you down into caves that spiral thousands of feet underground and you see extraordinary things. The guide warns everyone not to veer from the path because they will occasionally turn off the lights to show visitors what it is like to be in absolute darkness. As a child, my family visited the caves and I still to this day remember when they turned out all the lights. And as the old phrase says, I literally could not see my hand in front of my face. Likewise, in this spiritual state, you lose all sense of direction because you are totally without sight. This is a picture of how we are prior to getting saved, in that we are blinded to God. In fact, Galatians 4:8 tells us that prior to salvation we "served those which by nature are not gods." In this state, we will commit sins and we won't even consider the repercussions or the enormity of the repercussions. This is where we actually have difficulty seeing anything wrong with what was once a black and white decision.

It is a real tragedy when Christians come to the point where they are totally blind to the consequences of the sin they are in. Even in the act of adultery, they are not considering how much pain they will cause their spouse or their children or their church. Nobody reaches Step 3 without starting out at Step 1. It is a gradual downfall. Our understanding initially becomes darkened, and then we are blinded, and then we are existing in total darkness, unable to even see how to move. I hope you see the danger of allowing yourself to get to Step 1, because you are on a path that can lead to utter destruction.

Past Feeling

Some Bible versions use the term "being calloused," because when we reach this stage we become numb and lose the sense of feeling regarding our sin. As a child, I believed that people with leprosy had their limbs suddenly fall off. In reality, leprosy is a degenerative disease, which begins with numbing of the limbs and a loss of feeling in the nerve endings. Those afflicted with this terrible disease lose the capacity to feel with their hands and their body begins to self-destruct. Similarly, Christians who reach Step 4 are allowing their own actions to eat away at their very being. Scripture says of these people: "Their glory is their shame."

What a tragedy it is to see people literally self-destruct when they can't even feel the destruction within them. How do we get spiritually sick? We get numb. Worse, we rationalize this numbness and, even though we aren't reading our Bible and praying, we tell ourselves that we are as spiritually strong as ever because we go through perfunctory acts of liturgy every Sunday, and we've experienced spiritual growth in the past. But in the present, we are dying a slow spiritual death. We are rotting away. And worse, we are racing down the path to Step 5.

Lewdness

Other Bible versions use the word "sensuality" here. In the New Testament, the word for "lewdness" is a term that is coupled with drunkenness, sexual immorality and debauchery of any kind. The word describes an individual who is wallowing in carnality to such a point that it isn't even named among the Gentiles. Literally, the unbelieving community sees this action as being gross, nauseating, or disgusting. Here's an important point. If I were to ask you if you would like to participate in an act that would disgust me or anyone else you know, I'm sure you would say, "No." That's because to get to this point, people started at Step 1. But their spiritual digression brings them to this pitiful state. They began by trusting their own heart—instead of depending on the Mind of

Christ—and leaning on their own understanding. This points to the need for all of us to be constantly growing in Christ. We cannot remain babes in the faith forever because we will not gain the discernment and godly wisdom required to avoid arriving at Step 5. We must develop spiritual maturity. And so we traverse on to the final step.

Greediness

Yes, it gets worse than Step 5. At the end of verse 19, we read: "Greediness to work all uncleanliness with greediness." Those who reach this point do not mind if sin and sinful things are all that makes them feel good. They greedily want self-satisfaction and they don't care how they get it. Further, they don't mind profiting from sinful things. Christians at this point will participate in: pornography, drugs, crime, you name it. They will fill the void they have created within themselves with anything. And yet nothing will satisfy them.

In verse 20, we read: "But you have not so learned Christ." You haven't learned that your spiritual walk is down this path. Believers have you not seen the goodness of God and his protection? Why do we run away from the very source that will keep us from this spiritual destruction? Just two chapters earlier (Ephesians 2), Paul said, "In you God has made alive (those) who were dead in trespasses and sins ...." Why, after salvation, would we want to fall into the habits and lifestyle that characterized us prior to God redeeming us? Ephesians 2:4 describes God as being "rich in mercy," and verse 6 says that "He has raised us up." Our salvation is a gift from God, "not of your works." If left alone to our own works we would all arrive at Step 6. We are his workmanship created in Christ Jesus for good works which God prepared beforehand that we should walk in them" (Ephesians 2:10). We must always remember that, apart from Christ, we will destroy ourselves to the point of Step 6.

Watch Your Step

About six months ago, I had one of the scariest situations I've ever had as a parent. I was in the kitchen, and my daughter was about 3 ½ years old at the time. We had one of those multi-colored layered candles sitting on the island, and I could tell that my daughter's eye was attracted to the way the wax had become liquid surrounding the candle. I thought to myself that I would use this as a teachable moment, because it could be used anywhere. I went up to her and said, "Emma, look at that, it's pretty isn't it?" And she said, "Oh yeah, daddy, it is!!" And said, "But you can't touch, it's hot, hot, hot" as I reached toward the wax. I took my hand and put it over the candle and then took it away really quickly as I said, "It's hot, don't touch!" I don't know why I did this, but I started carrying on with things around the house, and before I knew it, I had left her there, and was heading down the hall when I heard the loudest scream, "Ouch, daddy, HOT!!!!" I ran back down toward the kitchen, and didn't see what I expected. No stools were overturned, and no spilled wax on the island, but there stood Emma two feet away with her hand stretched out toward the candle, and she was yelling, "Hot, hot, hot…it hurts the baby, daddy??" I looked to see if her hand had been hurt. There were no calluses, no ruin marks, and no blisters. Her hand was so tender; she could feel the heat from two feet away.

Our lives should be like her little hand. Unfortunately, our lives have become so calloused. Some of us can put our hands in the fire, we dip our fingers in the wax, we can come so close to the heat; yet our hands should be so tender, so sensitive to the baby steps of sin that we feel the pain, we know where it's going, and we run.

Write It Down

Unlike a roller coaster, in our spiritual walk, we can jump off. We have the ability, according to Romans 8, to be more than conquerors. What are some baby steps of sin that you have found yourself in, that if dealt with now could prevent you from going down the six-fold path as mention in Ephesians 4?

_____

_____

_____

_____

_____

_____

_____

_____

_____

_____

Take some time to listen to God's voice speaking to you in the area of sin in your life. As you feel led, spend the next few minutes writing out a prayer to the Lord dealing with what He's brought to your heart's attention.

_____

_____

_____

_____

_____

_____

_____

_____

_____

_____

_____

_____

_____

_____

_____

_____

_____

_____

Notes

CHAPTER FIVE

Walk In Grace

My father was a self-trained pastor. He was so passionate about ministry. I remember watching him, after his Sunday School class and after the church service at the alter, he would often give counsel, and I was so impressed. I wanted to be that type of person that was able to give advice. He listened so patiently, he comforted with such tenderness, and transparency. I would look at him and think it would take me years to develop his gift. I wanted to be like my father.

A few years down the road, I was contemplating Bible schools for college, and I was invited to a meet and greet for potential freshmen at a school close to where I lived in Michigan. The president of the college stood up and shared a verse that will forever stick with me; 1 Peter 3:15. "But sanctify the Lord God in your hearts, and always be ready to give a defense to everyone who asks you a reason for the hope that is in you, with meekness and fear." I thought to myself, that's what I want! That is the biblical sentence that articulates exactly what my heart has always wanted. I've always wanted to give guidance to people so that they would know how to live. Based on Truth, they would experience comfort; they would know that I care for them, and they would feel equipped and empowered to do the work of the ministry.

I thought there's no way I could achieve this level, because you have to be smart, you have to have degrees, and know the languages to help counsel people in the right direction. Not so, according to this verse. And not so according to the passage I will refer to in this chapter. You will see that any man or any woman who follows the prescriptions given from this passage can give spiritual counsel to anyone.

What If I'm Spiritually Sick?

When we are spiritually sick, we must reach a point where we recognize that we have become, first spiritually weak, and second sick. This passage in James 5:13-18 is one of the key segments of Scripture I utilize when counseling others on how to regain their spiritual strength. As we examine this passage, I want you to look for a familiar theme. I'll give you a hint; it is a word that is seen in every verse, and even twice in one of the verses.

Three Spiritual Diagnoses & Three Spiritual Prescriptions

When you are spiritually sick, prayer is the therapeutic spiritual medicine that brings about healing. Prayer is the balm on our spiritually weakened souls. I want to suggest that every aspect of these verses in James deal with our spiritual condition, and not a physical condition. For example, when verse 15 says, "The prayer of faith will save the sick," I believe this is referring to spiritual sickness. In other words, if you're in tune with the will of God, when you pray for someone your prayer can result in the healing of a spiritually sick person. Others see this as referring to physical sickness, but we know that Paul pleaded and prayed for a thorn of some sort of affliction to be removed, but God told him that He would not remove it. I think if we understand this entire passage as referring to spiritual weakness and the spiritual condition, it unites very beautifully. So that will be my perspective on this passage. Verses 13-14 provide the spiritual diagnosis, with James describing our spiritual condition as falling into one of three categories.

Afflicted..."let him pray" (v.13)

James uses an interesting word for "afflicted." This word in the Greek New Testament is used 50-50 in describing the spiritually and physically sick. It can mean physical ailments or spiritual weakness. When we think of someone who is spiritually afflicted we might think of someone who has been in a battle and is getting back up even though they are badly beaten up. It's like a prizefighter that gets knocked down but has enough strength to crawl up again. James is asking in verse 13, "Are any of you afflicted? Are any of you getting beat up spiritually? This may be describing you. Maybe you are "beaten up" because of family problems or school problems or relationship problems. And you've been knocked to the mat, so to speak, but you are trying to be strong and you're attempting to get back up by making this claim, "I know God's Word is true and I know He is good and I must get up. His way is the best way and I must follow Him instead of lying here in defeat." But it's hard to get up. Be ever mindful that God says, if you are afflicted, you have a prescription, "let him pray." This is a continuous action, meaning you don't just say a little prayer and hope things get suddenly better. You must continually be in the state of prayer; your lifeline to Christ must not become stifled. Spiritually, we can't become like a knotted hose that will not permit the water to flow through it. Christ wants to flow through us, especially when we are defeated and beaten up. He wants us to keep the prayer line open. Don't sever it; don't allow anything to stop that flow of prayer. Our God wants to hear from us and minister to us.

Merry..."let him sing psalms" (v.13)

The diagnosis is, "Is anyone merry? Is anyone well in soul?" The funny thing here is that James is saying these words to a group of people who are being terribly persecuted. But he's telling them, even as you are getting beat up and treated badly, "You should praise!" *Psalto* literally means "sing Psalms." Your prescription is to praise, he is telling them and us. You know, when you praise God even when you are facing a deep trial, your praise will not only strengthen you, it will bolster the faith of those around you. You need to share your testimony with others to show them that God supplies your hope and your strength. We never know who around us is experiencing spiritual pain as bad as, or maybe even worse than, our own. And they may have forgotten that they need to praise God even as they are suffering. So never withhold your praise to God; never be ashamed of the fact that your heart wants to praise Him, even in your times of trial. I think you will see that your wholehearted praise will actually be contagious. I'm not talking about praise that is designed to garner man's applause—I'm talking about true, heartfelt praise that wells up inside of you because God is blessing you and working with you beyond your imagination. That kind of real praise can be a great encouragement to others who need to see it. As the old song says, "It is well with my soul." I know how much it encourages me when I am around someone who is well in his/her soul and I see the great praise springing forth from within. Never withhold your praises to God.

Sick..."call on the elders" (v.14)

In verse 14, the word used for "sick" is an interesting one, in that while it is occasionally used to describe physical ailments, it is mostly used to denote spiritual ailments. This word is used to describe someone who is being spiritually beaten up to the point that they haven't the strength to get up. Have you ever been to this place spiritually? It is a tough place to be. I have been beaten up so badly in my past that I reached a point that I didn't even want to pray. Listen, I understand that there are times in a Christian's life that our hearts become so spiritually sick that we are beside ourselves and we feel we can't even approach God with our pain or problems. You simply can't get your mind focused on spiritual things. I know from my counseling experiences, that people face many problems. You might have trouble in your home and your heart has become angry. Maybe you're struggling with a relationship issue. But there is a spiritual prescription for healing. Verse 14 tells us: "Let him call for the elders of the church ...." I want to share a couple of thoughts on what comes next in this passage.

Anoint them with oil

In the Greek language there is a pattern of speech or a grammatical element called a participle. In English, a participle is used for the most part in words ending in "ing." It is a descriptive word that uses an action verb step; for ex-

ample, laughing, praising, singing, teaching. The Apostle John frequently uses this form regarding Jesus (i.e., "living water). You could say, "pretty water," "clean water." Those are adjectives describing the water. But when you make your descriptive word an action word, like "running," you've flipped it into a participle.

In the Greek text, participles occur either before the main verb, after the main verb, or at the same time that the main verb is occurring. Our main verb phrase here is: "let them pray"—so our main verb is "pray." Some Bible versions say, "Let them pray over him after anointing him with oil," meaning we're putting the anointing idea first. So if you're dealing with someone that's spiritually bitter, angry, down for the count and can't even get up, as spiritual leaders and counselors and mentors we're to first anoint them and then pray for them. I know that the idea of anointing may seem strange to some. I have many friends and colleagues who perform anointing services. I fondly remember being anointed with oil following my doctoral graduation. Anointing with oil is a viable procedure that indicates through the action of placing oil on a person's head, we are trusting God to physically heal because no other human device and method has been successful. This procedure should not be taken lightly, as we are acknowledging God as the Great Healer. But, we said from the onset that this passage is referring to spiritual sickness and spiritual instability.

This word, *anoint*, is not the word for the anointing service or a liturgy. It is, rather, a word that means to massage or to rub, as you would take oil in your hands to give someone a back rub in order to soothe their aching muscles. I described earlier a brief occasion during which I could not pray. Have you ever been forced to your knees at a time when your heart was not ready to pray? Similarly, have you ever compelled someone to their knees even though they weren't in a condition to pray? I realize that we are programmed to say, "Let's drop to our knees and pray right now," and yet, sometimes people simply aren't ready to pray. This is a time when we must "massage" and encourage them to help them begin to recover their spiritual strength. We need to have discernment at these times. Philippians 1:9 says, "You can have discernment in all things." Ask God for wisdom and discernment during these times. In Luke 10:38-41, we see that sitting at the feet of Jesus can heal our anxieties and our spiritual pain.

Pray over them
After a season at His feet, we are then prepared in our hearts to return to prayer. Psalm 23 says, "The Lord is my shepherd." When King David was fourteen years of age, he was a shepherd. He would, like other shepherds, often administer oil on the sheep that had experienced cuts or bruises. He would set down his staff and allow the sheep to enter one at a time so that he could give them individual attention, rubbing a special oil on the sheep's parched

face, legs and feet. And then he would lift his rod and let another sheep come in and he would continue the practice, individually and lovingly ministering to each one. David, reflecting on his time as a shepherd, says these words, "You anoint my head with oil; my cup runs over." (Psalm 23) He is saying that God has taken care of him spiritually. He is saying that God has massaged his soul and now he longs to praise God who has brought this wonderful comfort. That is what James is saying here, "You have anointed my head with oil." If you are spiritually sick, you need to experience the balm of Christ. You need to experience a spiritual massage that will enable you to experience healing. And then you will be able to pray anew. And when we experience this special time with God, there are spiritual results. Let's examine them in the next section.

Spiritual Results

What are the results of regaining your spiritual strength? What are the results of experiencing a spiritual massage that enables you to love and pray again? Verse 15 lists three spiritual results, saying: "The prayer of faith will save the sick."

Prayer of faith will save the sick

This word saved (sodzo) is complete; there's nothing we can add to the translation. But there is an interesting note, depending on the context. The word "saved" in Scripture sometimes refers to being saved from a physical storm, while other times it refers to being spiritually saved. It's a word that has many contexts, but in a spiritual sense, it has great significance. In this context, it means to make whole or to complete. Notice what it says about the prayer of faith in the previous verse. If they pray and they truly want God to spiritually heal them, their prayer of faith will absolutely, positively be honored. You will never be left waiting when you ask God, "Can I be spiritually rich again? Can I be spiritually strong again?" The answer is always a resounding, "Yes!" If you want to be spiritually well again, the Lord has promised to make you whole.

The Lord will raise him up

If you want to be spiritually revived or restored, we read, "The Lord will raise him up." The word "raise" is the Greek word egeiro which is where we get our word for energy. We see here that God will energize or invigorate you again when you ask this of Him. How do we know this? Because it is His promise to do so! If you want to be spiritually well again, you must approach God and confess your weakness and your dependence on Him. Tell Him, "I want to be made whole again." He says He will save you and He will make you whole.

Sins will be confessed

He further promises to energize you spiritually. And this is a great point; He says, "If you have committed sins, they will be forgiven." I love the concrete statements, you will be whole, you will be raised up, and your confessed sins will be forgiven. This should encourage us all!

This is one of those interesting phrases that some people believe to be out of place or a little detached—a bit of a staccato statement. They ask, "Why talk about the confession of sin at this point when we are focusing on people getting raised up?" I believe this is a very important verse (v.14) because it is forcing us to see that our spiritual sickness is most likely, but not always attributable to our sin. Therefore, we see that our spiritual sickness is typically a self-inflicted affliction. We bring it on ourselves because of and through our sin. In verse 15, we see that if you're made whole and spiritually energized again, it is because your sin has been confessed and wiped away. It should not haunt you anymore or drive you into spiritual sickness. This is a beautiful verse because we see here that the Lord will save the spiritually weary. God does not condemn you when you become weary; He simply wants to forgive your sin, lift you up and make you spiritually whole again.

Preventive Medicine
Verse 16 is about preventive medicine, spiritually speaking. It's a wonderful passage because we, as believers who have the propensity of falling into spiritual sickness, need to "confess our sins." Incidentally, there should be the word 'therefore' beginning in v. 16. The KJV doesn't have it, while the ESV and the NIV do have it. The little Greek word "*oun*", or therefore, is important because it builds on everything else. It is saying this, "Therefore, despite the fact that I can get spiritually sick and there may be a time I don't feel like praying, there is a preventive medicine." It is saying, "Therefore confess your," and the word is "sins" in the Greek, "sins one to another and pray for one another that you may be healed." In modern language, this passage is describing what we call accountability. This is a very important part of the Christian life that we need to investigate.

Accountability needed

Sin wants you to isolate yourself. Sin wants you to be hidden. But when we have an accountability partner—a person who wants to help us remain spiritually strong and focused on the mind of Christ—we are compelled to come out of spiritual isolation. This friend wants to help us stay in the Word of God, refrain from falling into old habits, and keep us from falling into a spiral of spiritual sickness. This is a person who knows you, understands you, and recognizes the signs that you might be spiritually struggling. The word confess, (exomologeo), is interesting and unique. It's not the same word we see in 1 John 1:9 ("If we confess our sin..."). That Greek word is homologeo and it means to openly aknowledge your sins one to another (meaning another believer).

You will not be able to have strong spiritual accountability and counsel if you are depending on a non-believer to help you with accountability. I pray that you will find an accountability partner you can value and upon whom you can depend and trust. 1 Corinthians says that the preaching of the gospel is foolishness to those that don't believe. Even the most well intentioned non-believer cannot understand spiritual truths.

From a righteous person

Prayer needed

In addition to finding accountability, we also need prayer. We read, "The effectual fervent prayer from a righteous man...." This is part of sharing in someone's accountability. Your accountability partner should be righteous and holy; someone who is not spiritually sick himself/herself, because misery loves company. A spiritually sick person cannot help you out of your own spiritual sickness. It should be someone you can pray with that you know to be attuned to the mind of Christ. This will continually empower you and encourage you.

From a passionate heart

We must be prayed for passionately, through a heart that loves and sees the value of prayer. "The effectual fervent prayer of a righteous man," the Greek says, "is very powerful." There is such a thing, as someone offering a weak prayer, and they can affect many people. In fact, if we are involved in a sinful lifestyle, this can affect the entire body of Christ. Never believe the lie that some people depend on, "My sin is between me and God and has nothing to do with you." Well, according to this verse, your prayers for me should be powerful; the only way your prayers will be powerful is if you're living a righteous life. So we see that even the most secret and sealed sin can affect the body of Christ. Your sin can affect me; my sin can affect you. But listen, if you are a righteous man or woman who is pursuing the heart of God, your prayers can bring down the heavens!

An Old Testament Comparison (v. 17-18)

This passage ends in two verses, and makes a comparison. Some have wondered why the prophet Elijah is mentioned here. James is summing up his teaching like a good pastor might do at the end of his sermon. He's wrapping it up with what he sees as the most vivid and powerful example, and as a Jew, he recalls Elijah—one of the most fanciful and romantic of the prophets. In fact, Elijah is no doubt his Old Testament hero. Elijah, you see, was a man very similar to us, even though he is remembered as a great prophet. He prayed with great power. In fact, he prayed that it wouldn't rain, and didn't rain on the earth for a space of three years and six months. The New Testament writers loved Elijah. To show how much they loved him, when Jesus asked, "Who do men say that I am?" they replied, "Some say you are Elijah." James said, "Yes and Elijah prayed and it didn't rain on the earth for three years six months and he prayed again and the heaven gave rain and the earth brought forth her fruit!"

Here's the point; James was saying that the prayers of all believers are so powerful they too can bring rain and spiritual nourishment to a dry, parched soul and that soul can bear fruit again. Yes, Elijah was a great man, but he was also just like us. You too can pray with the same power and bring life-changing support to fellow believers.

Where are you today spiritually? Are you prepared to offer prayers like Elijah? I don't believe you can progress any further in this study without first looking at your own heart and determining the state of your spiritual health. True success in Christian service and ministry comes only when your heart is purified before God and your efforts are holy and righteous and pure.

write It Down

Are you spiritually sick? If so, where do you see yourself according to the three diagnosis mentioned at the beginning of this chapter?

_____

_____

_____

_____

_____

_____

_____

_____

_____

_____

As a believer, if you are spiritually healthy, are you providing accountability and prayer to those who are your brothers and sisters in Christ? Explain how this is going and/or how it is being received.

_____

_____

_____

_____

_____

_____

_____

_____

_____

_____

_____

_____

_____

_____

_____

_____

_____

_____

_____

Notes

Respond

CHAPTER SIX

Serve Others

Before we can talk about evangelistic efforts and articulating our faith to others, we must first focus on the condition of our hearts. You see if we are not in line with the Holy Spirit our efforts will be empty and ultimately fruitless.

I recently had an individual approach me, and I remember vividly what he said, "If someone needs to get on fire for God, wouldn't it be beneficial to get him involved in ministry or in a leadership role, and then he could taste and see that the Lord is good?" The only thing that came to mind when he raised this question was this – the person was essentially saying that it might be profitable to put someone in a church "doing position" or service position without them having a heart that is prepared for servitude. I believe that's a prescription for failure. Scripture makes it very clear that prior to doing the work of ministry, we must first be spiritually prepared for such ministry.

In Acts 6:3; we see where the disciples were instructed by Paul to meet the needs of widows. He stated, "Would you gather among you seven faithful men filled with the Holy Ghost and then we will deal with this business at hand." Prior to dealing with the business at hand the men needed to be spiritual, controlled, and in line with God. Before they could "do," they needed to be ready.

I also think of 2 Timothy 2:2 where Paul says, "Timothy, commit these things to faithful men. Don't commit these things in order to make them faithful, but find men who are committed, who are spiritually mature and then commit these things to them." He wanted them to mentor men who were already somewhat mature, or men who saw their need for spiritual growth.

By examining these passages we see that we, as Christians today, need to be similarly prepared to do ministry. Therefore, I don't want to jump right into evangelism without first addressing who we should be. This is a very important element of Christian service.

65

I was told at the first Bible college I attended that our personal devotion time should be comprised of material outside of our class studies and that we should take time to talk to godly men who could influence our walk with Christ. One author of more than forty books who came to our school (the late John Wolford) made this statement, "I do not find myself getting the most out of God's word unless I'm preparing to write a book, or preparing to preach a sermon or a lesson." He was saying, "If I'm not studying for a purpose it's hard to get something out of it." I agreed with him that I should make my studies my devotion, studying for knowledge, applcation, and life-change.

For you, I think the Lord has seen fit to put the subjects of evangelism and the Christian life in your life, and I pray that you will be able to use these times of examination of God's Word, as a personal devotion and a time of examining your heart. In fact, if your mind is truly meditating on these spiritual truths, I believe you will learn great ways to apply these principles to your life and also how to infuse your heart with His precious Word.

Before I Do, I Must Be

There are many misconceptions about what a godly person is. Many people refer to others as being "spiritual". For example I have heard students recommend a girl to a friend as a potential date because "she's really a godly person." Or you may hear someone saying, "You ought to consider dating him because he really loves the Lord." However, it is a likely possibility that the person being recommended is not a godly person in the true sense.

We are going to search God's Word and look at what a godly person truly is, because we, as believers, need to make sure we understand what it means to be a godly person, and we, as believers, need to desire to be holy before God.

Misconceptions About Being a Godly Person

They have biblical training (Isaiah 29:13)
Some people will say a godly person is one who has received Bible training. Let's look at Isaiah 29:13: "*Wherefore the Lord said, for as much as this people draw near to me with their mouth; with their lips they honor me, but have moved their heart from me and their fear towards me is taught by the precepts of men.*" Let me paraphrase: "They know a lot about me and do lip service to me, but their hearts are moved from me because"—and let me utilize the NIV here—"their reverence for me was learned by the tradition of rote memory." Literally, they have learned my precepts by empty rote memorization and have essentially flash carded God's attributes to death without their heart being linked in devotion to God.

The English Standard Version says, "The Lord says my people draw near me with their mouth, their lips honor me, but their hearts are far from me, their fear of me is a commandment that is simply taught to them by men." Many people sit through years of Sunday school classes; they know the stories in their heads but do not apply them to their hearts. They may have a perfect church attendance, they may have earned badges and memorized verses, but this usually will not produce a godly person in and of itself. It's all for show. The truths of God must be received into the heart and then lived out.

I was at a men's retreat in Jonesboro, Georgia with a fellow pastor, talking about integrity and purity among the men there. In a Q&A session the pastor and I lead, one of the men asked: "How is it that some pastors who preach the Word week in and week out can fall into adultery?" I responded: "I believe it's often because those pastors prepare sermons in second and third person. They say 'he' must do this, 'the church' must do that, and 'you' must do this. But prior to preaching, he needs to speak it in first person. He must say, 'I' must do this, or how can 'I' conform my life to this portion of God's Word?" Pastors and trained Bible students will fail when their training is all for show. They are just going through the routine or going through the motions. You see, if you tout how many books and volumes you have on your shelf but your heart is not holy, then the books are mere showpieces. So we see that it is not biblical training that necessarily prepares a person to be "godly." So it must be something else.

They attend church (Matthew 17)
In Matthew chapter 17 we read that on Judgment Day, many will say, "Lord, Lord we've done many things in your name!" And they will name off all the things—many of them good things—they did for God. I know this passage is somewhat debatable because some say these people are believers, while some say they are not. If they are believers, they've done incredibly spiritual things: performing miracles, casting out demons, etc. Yet, the Bible says the Lord will say to them, "Depart from me; I never knew you." Some suggest these people are unbelievers who hung around in church and knew how to use the Christian vernacular in an attempt to persuade God to let them into heaven. They "talk the talk" but it's all empty.

Regardless of who these individuals are, we see through their example that we must achieve more than a mere understanding of God; we must have more than a mere cognitive knowledge of Him. It's not just individuals that know the ways of Christianity. There is a saying that twenty percent of the church does eighty percent of the work. We typically view the twenty percent as godly people, but a godly person must be about more than just work.

In the Third Epistle of John, we see the story of a guy named Diotrephes. John says in 3 John verse 9, "*I wrote to the church, but Diotrephes who loves to have the pre-eminence (first place) in the church, did not receive us.*" We don't know if this man was a pastor or not, but we know he wanted to be; he wanted to be the leader.

In Colossians 1:18, we are told that, "Jesus Christ is the head of the church, He is the beginning, He is the first born from the dead that in all things He he will have the preeminence (first place)." If you want first place in the church solely for your own glory, you're going toe-to-toe with Jesus Christ. And so we see that Diotrephes was off track. Deeds performed in church or profound actions do not gain prominence with God.

In Matthew 13 we read the parable of the four soils. Seed is thrown on soil and some of it takes root and is then snatched away, some hits bedrock and dies, some is trampled on and there is no growth, and some hits the fine soil. These examples of soil represent non-believers. In like manner, some people show the likeness of a true believer but have no true grounding so that when things get tough they wither away.

Spiritual Parents

Another misconception is that if we have spiritual parents we too will be automatically spiritual. I recall after my wife and I got married, she was sharing the gospel with a woman who was not a believer yet she said, "Oh, I'm going to heaven." My wife replied, "Really? How do you know you're on your way to heaven?" The woman said, "Because my mother washes the parish priest's robes every week, and it takes a very special person to do this." My wife found her responses sad as she was relying on her mother to gain spirituality.

In Philippians 3:4-5, Paul addressed this type of belief when he said, "If anyone thinks they should have more confidence in their flesh I can beat them. I was circumcised the eighth day. I was a legitimate Jew as far as circumcision. Stock of Israel, Tribe of Benjamin, a Hebrew of Hebrews." This is a comment about his family and their wealth and standing in the Jewish community. The best teacher in Tarsus, Gamelial, educated him. But then Paul goes on to say, "But what things were gain to me those I count as loss for Christ."

Paul considered and weighed the worth of all that he had and all that he was and, like an accountant weighing assets and liabilities, no longer considered them an asset, but considered them of no worth in comparison to knowing Christ. So as we are weighing these different things: biblical training, church attendance, and spiritual parents, and find that it is not these things which make a person godly in and of themselves, we see the need to continue on in our biblical search for the description of a godly person.

A Biblical Description

"The primary goal of biblical education is to produce a person who is self-disciplined in godly attitudes and habits!" (The International Standard Bible Encyclopedia)

As we learn about God, His Word and His Church through biblical education and training, the goal is to produce a person who is self-disciplined in godly attitudes and habit. A person, who takes the truth of God's Word and consistently lives it out day-by-day, from the heart, being careful to obey it. That is a godly person.

An Analogy

You're sitting in church, listening to a sermon on Luke 7. In the middle of this chapter, you hear a story about a funeral procession wherein a widow is burying her only son. The preacher reminds you that in Jewish culture this woman is in the most despairing situation because if you are a widow and you have lost your only son, this means you have no males to protect or support you. You further learn that this is why a great company from the town is with her. You hear that Jesus walks up to this woman and says, "Don't cry." Your intellect is spurred a little bit; you're stimulated intellectually by all of these little facts. You conclude: "I've learned something new. I've been fed. Therefore, I'm spiritual!" No way. You've just learned some biblical facts that have stimulated you intellectually. And then consider Jesus' words to the widow: "Don't cry." And you think, in tough times I don't have to cry because Christ is with me and will take care of things. You say, "I've made an application and drafted the application. Therefore, I'm spiritual!" Nope. You've simply made a logical deduction. So you continue to forge an opinion, "When times get tough I will trust Christ. Great—I've more than applied this truth. I have prepared myself for the reaction I should have. Therefore, I'm spiritual!" No, again. You have simply added another "go to" reaction on the flow chart of your mind.

Here is the proper application. When times are tough, you trust Him. And then you run into another tough time and you trust Him. And yet another tough time comes and you still proclaim, "I have seen the goodness of God and I will never leave Him. I know He is always with me. He is good and kind and loving and merciful and compassionate and has never winked at my plight; He has never slumbered at my request. I will and I must trust Him again and again no matter how difficult life becomes." That is the committed faith of a person who is self-disciplined in godly attitudes and habits.

You may be like me. When tough times come, there's an inner battle. Tough times come and you struggle within yourself and think, "Why am I struggling like this?" A truly godly person is someone who is self-disciplined, whose default reaction is saying, "I will follow God's way, no matter what."

Allow me to share a personal note. Let me tell you what I do when the Evil One comes with his temptations. I know my flesh well enough to know that I cannot battle against these temptations by myself. My flesh needs an insertion of truth that cuts through my own faulty logic and limitations. So when I face temptation or I struggle spiritually, I often say aloud: "God's way; God's way; God's way!" And as I'm saying this, I slowly begin to see through new eyes. I have learned that our flesh will not want to pursue righteousness. Therefore, we must defeat the cravings of sin before they take root within us. And so in my own weakness, I call out to my Lord by claiming "God's way" over and over. In so doing, I disrupt the flow of the flesh. This is my personal act of self-discipline, as I call on God to help me avoid temptation. A two-fold way to becoming a godly person is: (1) recognize your weakness amid temptation and (2) call on God, maybe even verbally, when you are struggling with temptation or discouragement or disbelief. I pray you always live life God's way, God's way, God's way!

A Look At Your Own Heart - Psalm 139

I think it is vitally important that we take critical looks at our own hearts from time to time. My favorite Psalm is chapter 139, which I believe is the most beautiful of Psalms. It provides guidance in the examination of our hearts. Verses 1-6 read: "Oh Lord, You have searched me and known me. You know my sitting down and my rising up; You understand my thoughts afar off. You comprehend my path and my lying down, and are acquainted with all my ways. For there is not a word on my tongue, but behold, O Lord, You know it altogether. You have hedged me behind and before, and laid Your hand upon me. Such knowledge is too wonderful for me; it is high, I cannot attain it."

> **Verse 1**—You've searched me and know me
> **Verse 2**—You know my sitting down, You understand my thought
> **Verse 3**—You comprehend my path, You are acquainted with my ways
> **Verse 4**—There is not a word on my tongue, but oh Lord You know it altogether.
> **Verse 6**—Such knowledge is too wonderful for me.

Then in verses 7-12, David speaks of God's omnipresence. He says: "Where can I go from Your spirit? Where can I flee from Your presence?"

> **Verse 8**—If I make my bed in the grave You are there
> **Verse 9**—If I take—and listen to the Jewish mindset here, the figurative language— the wings of the morning (as quick as the morning creeps up on us) and I dwell (or I shoot) right into the uttermost parts of the sea, even there will Your hand lead me and Your right hand will hold me. If you know the geography of the Jewish nation of Jerusalem, then you know the sun rises in the east. In Jewish geography to their

west is the Mediterranean Sea, so to say as quick as the wings of the morning comes (east) and I shoot in the farthest corner of the sea (west), even there Your hand leads me Your right hand will hold me.
Verse 11—If I say the darkness will cover me, the darkness is like light around me
Verse 12—The darkness shall not hide from You, but the night shines like the day. The darkness and the light, they're both alike to You. I can't hide from You.

Not being able to hide from God shouldn't be a scary thing. The fact that God knows you through and through should be reassuring to you. I remember in elementary school, if I had a bad report card I was fearful. But bringing home a positive report card for my parents was exciting. Likewise, if our lives are holy we welcome God fully knowing us. Conversely, if our life has sin it in, like 1 John says, "He is light and in Him there is no darkness at all," then, it's a scary thing. A godly person begs to be transparent and loves God's scrutiny. Your spiritual stability is in direct proportion to how you view God.

Verses 13-16 talk about God's omnipotence; the fact that God is all powerful.

Verse 13—You have possessed, or formed, my range. You have covered me, or knitted me together in my mother's womb. I will praise You for I am fearfully and wonderfully made. Marvelous are Thy works and I know it very well.
Verse 15—My substance was not hidden from Thee me when I was secretly and intricately made in the lowest parts of the earth. Your eye saw my substance even though I wasn't made yet. All the members of me were written in the book when there weren't any at the time.
Verse 17—How precious are thy thoughts unto me oh God? How great is the sum of them? If I should count them they are more in number than the sand. This great God that knows me is everywhere with me; is powerful to protect and create me; loves me.
Verse 19—Oh that You would slay the wicked, oh God. Depart from me you bloody men. For they speak against You wickedly and Your enemies take Thy name in vain. Do I not hate them that hate thee oh Lord? And do I not loathe those that rise up against You? I hate them with perfect hatred; I count them my enemies.

You think, "Whoa, that's not a psalm of love!" It is important to see that David is saying, "You are a great God that knows all and is everywhere and is so powerful and Your thoughts upon us are numerous, even more than the granules on the beach." And he continues: "I love You and it grieves me when people don't." And he's literally saying, "Please, as you look upon me, see me differently than

You do those who blaspheme You. I don't want anything to do with those that are blaspheming You. I don't want to be in their company." Psalm 1 says, *"Blessed is the man that walks not in the counsel of the ungodly, nor stands in the way of sinners nor sits in the seat of the scornful, but his delight is in the law of the Lord and in His law does he meditate day and night."* I don't want anything in my life that will align me with such people, and I want to separate everything I do from those that blaspheme God. I want to protect my Christian reputation.

Then in Verse 23, it says, *"search me oh God and know my heart; try me and know my anxieties. See if there is any wicked way in me and lead me in the way everlasting."*

A Willing Submission To His Ways

In verse 1, David makes the statement, "Lord You have searched me and You know me." Why in the world, if God has searched him and has known him, is he then in verse 23 asking God to please search him and know his heart and to try him and know his thoughts? Hasn't God already done this? Doesn't that seem somewhat odd? This is the sign of a strong spiritual man because David is expressing a willing submission to God's ways all the time. He is saying, "God, I know You already do this, but I want to show You that I'm going to go with You willingly and I welcome You to search my heart."

When police officers come to the point where they are going to have to take an individual into custody, they ask, "Are you going to cooperate with us or do we have to take you by force?" This is the same concept. God searches us. He knows us, but it's the heart that says, "You are a good God; You know me and I want to know You" (Psalm 3:10). We must welcome His presence and His searching of our hearts. I want to know God and I want to say to Him, "I'm going to go with you everywhere." That is the heart that is willing and open to Christ. Are you a godly person? Am I a godly person, I ask myself? The answer lies in this question: Am I willing to go God's way and am I willing to open my heart to Him at all times?

How Important Is My Relationship To Jesus?

If we love righteousness we will pursue it. If we find joy in the study of God's Word and the life change it brings in our hearts, we will crave righteousness. It's the things that we do grudgingly that will not, after a while, be true of us. A man will go shopping with his wife who will visit many stores that hold no interest at all for him. It is exhausting to most men! And the typical man will sit while his wife tries on clothes and he's almost lazy-eyed he's so tired and then one of his buddies will call on the phone and say, "Hey, you want to come over and watch ESPN and order some pizza?" And the husband replies, "Yeah!" But his wife says, "I thought you were tired and you wanted to go home." "Well I just got a burst of energy," the husband says sheepishly. This is a picture of our heart with God many times. We will do what we love to do and if our relationship to Jesus is something we value we'll pursue God's way. That is the heart of a godly Christian.

John 14:1-3 is one of the last words that Jesus shared before making His way to the Garden of Gethsamane prior to His crucifixion. He said, "*Let not your heart be troubled, you believe in God believe also in Me. In my father's house there are many mansions, if it were not so I would have told you. I go to prepare a place for you and I will come again and receive you unto Myself that where I am there may you be also.*"

You may ask, how does this have anything to do with how important my relationship is with Jesus? In John 14, the disciples are in the upper room having the last Passover meal and Jesus is telling them that one of them will betray Him soon. It is unthinkable to the other eleven. And they respond: "Is it me?" None of them say, "Is it Judas?" You see, he had disguised himself so well among them and they never suspected that it would be him. Then Jesus dipped in the sop and turned to Judas, saying, "What thou doest, doest quickly." Judas left, with the others believing he was getting food for the Passover. Then Jesus turns to His disciples and shares these encouraging words, "Don't be troubled. You believe in God you must believe in Me...." Jesus is telling His disciples that He is credible, considerate, and compassionate. Further, He gives them a little character sketch and reminds them of how much He loves them.

Just like Psalm 139, and using the same words to describe His character, Jesus conveys to them what He needs to see in their character. In essence, He was telling them, "I need to see faithfulness from you. If you committed your heart to Me, I need you to be faithful."

Jesus then draws an analogy to a Jewish marriage ceremony, literally describing how a man gets engaged. You see, a Jewish man, if he wanted to be engaged to and marry a woman, would find her and take her and his own dad to visit the woman's dad. The young man would turn to the father of the woman and say, "I want to marry your daughter." And the father would say, "Fine, but it will cost you." And they would negotiate all that the groom-to-be would have to provide for the bride; they called it a bride price. He would work a certain amount of years, give his father-in-law livestock, and promise him certain possessions. In fact the bride price would rival the price of a middle-class home. The father of the bride would finally stop negotiations and agree that this bride price was sufficient. He would take a cup of wine and he would put it to his lips stating that he accepts the bride price if the groom chooses to pay it. He would then give the cup of wine to the groom and if the groom put it to his lips, he was saying he agreed to pay the bride price. Then the groom would turn to the young woman and extend the cup toward her and say, "This is the cup of my new covenant; will you drink?" And she had two options: (1) reject the cup or (2) put it to her lips, indicating that she was accepting the bride price. If she chose option 2, the couple was espoused, immediately. It would take a write of divorce to break this bond. Interestingly, they would have a very small meal together at this time and not a big ceremony.

Afterward, the young man and his family would bid the bride and her family farewell and leave for about a period of twelve months. He would leave and go back to his father's home where he would immediately begin renovations. He would extend the father's home and think about what his bride would like and he would fix up the courtyard and do many things over the course of a year before his bride came to live there. During this period, she has ceased her responsibilities. Along with her mother and other married women, she would fashion her whole heart and her entire life and mind for married life with her soon-to-be husband. She would look at different portions of the writings and teachings in order to learn how to be a godly woman. And when the period of 12 months were done, the groom would dress in white and make a trek toward the city.

As the young man approached, from rooftop to rooftop people would shout, "He's coming! He's coming!" Then the young man would arrive at her door and the shouts would continue: "He's coming!" She would dress in white, and stand with her bridesmaids. He would stand away from the door and with a shofar horn, he'd blow and she'd come out the door. And he would take her by the hand and take her back to his father's house. They would have a seven-day festival, a tradition wherein she was veiled. And after the seven days they would raise the veil so everyone could see who the bride was.

In the middle of this Passover meal in order to calm the disciples, Jesus says, "Let not your heart be troubled …." He was essentially saying, "I'm leaving, but I'm coming back for you as a groom will return for his bride. Know that My heart, My mind, and My thoughts are on you. I love you; how precious are My thoughts unto you."

Application

Today, we stand right where the bride and disciples did. And Jesus is saying to us, "While I'm gone, be faithful to me." In fact if the bride, during that year was to be unfaithful the man would have to divorce her, without option. In fact, that's where Mary and Joseph were—they were apart and Joseph was away when he heard that Mary was with child and he was going to divorce her privately.

But the angel interrupted and said, "No, it's the Holy Ghost who is the Father." Today, we are standing as the bride, having to fashion our entire minds, our hearts, our entire lives for "married life" with Him.

I think of 2 Corinthians 11:2-3, "*For I am jealous for you with a godly jealousy; for I betrothed you to one husband, so that to Christ I might present you as a pure virgin. But I am afraid that, as the serpent deceived Eve by his craftiness, your minds will be led astray from the simplicity and purity of devotion to Christ.*" In other words, some of us cheat on God. Where are you? How valuable is your relationship to Jesus? How precious is it that you are a person that is self-disciplined with godly attitudes and habits. Every time we take the cup of communion, we remember not only the blood of Christ that was shed for us and not only His body that was broken. We remember also the new covenant. Remember Paul's words in Corinthians: "This is the cup of my new covenant." Jesus stood at the last Passover meal, and said, "This is the cup of My new covenant." He reminds us that we have committed our lives to Him.

And so we see that before we can talk about evangelizing, we must first talk about our own hearts and how we represent God to the world.

write It Down

Are you a godly person? Is your "default reaction" one of obedience to the Holy One? How does this relate to serving others?

How are you preparing for "married life" with Jesus according to the analogy used in John 14?

_____

_____

_____

_____

_____

_____

_____

_____

_____

_____

_____

_____

_____

_____

_____

_____

Notes

CHAPTER SEVEN

Share with others

Nothing will instill a doctrine, life-lesson, principle, or skill into a person's mind more than having to teach it to someone else. Teaching forces a person to not only study a particular topic so that they comprehend it, but to present it in such a way that others can comprehend it as well.

The same is true in the development of our spiritual lives. Spending time reading the Bible and other writings is indeed a great start, but a person can better instill in themselves biblical truths by also teaching or sharing these truths with others. This chapter has been written to suggest how you can practically share the truths of the gospel, that you yourself are learning, with others.

The manner in which we present the gospel may vary depending on the audience; however, the message must remain the same. For instance, the way I present the gospel to a child would be different from the way I would present the gospel to an unsaved adult. We must be careful to never compromise the truth for the sake of the audience. We cannot skew any fact of the gospel, or leave out any detail regardless of the individual, environment, or scenario.

With my biblical studies students, I attempt to help them learn to exercise their ability to convert theological definitions into a language a four year old could comprehend by assigning them a word like the word *sanctification*. I will give them fifteen minutes to discuss it amongst themselves then ask them to demonstrate how they would speak to the four year old. One stipulation is that they cannot cut corners on the truth.

I will give another group the word heart. I tell them the heart is the center and seat of emotion, the very decision force within us, the center of our will. Then I tell them to demonstrate how they would explain that to a four year old. The mind of a child and their innocence is fascinating. A pastor once told me that a man in his congregation had a heart transplant and he had a child in the group go up to the man and ask him if he needed to ask Jesus into his heart again. Of course that's sweet; you can picture a child saying that. Obviously, there's a deeper meaning. When we ask Jesus into our heart we are asking Him to infuse that decision into our heart, into the center and seat of our emotion and intellect, into our very being.

Unfortunately, I believe in our current society some are more interested in the presentation than the truth of what is being presented. Jesus himself, all throughout the gospels, was very cognizant of how he presented truth to individuals. He too seemed to feel that presentation was important. For example, in talking about giving alms, He brought up nuances about the theater. He says (paraphrase), "Your right hand shouldn't know what your left hand is doing, but you guys would rather parade and blow trumpets as you give your alms." And that's a picture of the theater. Key actors would walk through the main road of the city to the theater and they would applaud and blow trumpets, and that was the way He related to them. I think the presentation is very important. I am all about being creative. In fact, the more creative tools to attract the listener the better. However, the ultimate goal is to preach the unadulterated gospel, so I just want to briefly talk about the manner in which we convey these truths.

Be Ready

The manner in which we present the truths of the biblical teaching of salvation is definitely addressed in scripture, and I think it is very important to highlight these. Various verses in the Bible speak to how we should share the gospel. I want you to view these few verses as different tools in a tool belt. If you are anything like me, I call my father or friends around me to do work for me; I am not a handy man by any means. These guys that help me out don their tool belt with all of these tools, and when they approach a certain job or task they look around and grab the right tool and do the job. They will not waste time running to the other side of the house to grab another tool. They think all of their tools "on the ready." I think it would be a little ridiculous if we hired a handy man and he only had one tool on his tool belt, and for every single job he applied that one tool. Likewise, I want you to look at these different methods as different tools. There may be an occasion where you are more forceful, but then there may be times where you can simply converse with a person. Let's take a look at a few methods.

1 Peter 3:15 says, "But sanctify the Lord God in your hearts and be ready always to give an answer." It's this word *answer* that is really interesting. There are many ways to give answers and respond. You can respond militarily, competitively, angrily, or passively. In Scripture there are different ways to give an answer as well. In the book of Colossians, Paul answers back some opponents polemically, which means to wage war. You can understand why he would

do that because they are saying that Jesus Christ is not God. They were just saying that he's just a nice angel, but He and every other angel must be worshipped, but He is not really God; nor is He sufficient for salvation. So Paul is very polemic and in chapter 1, verse 5 and following he says, "He (Christ) is the head of the church. He is the image of the invisible God. He is the firstborn of all Creation, for by Him all things are created that are in heaven and that are in earth...." Very specific and very bold. In 1 Peter 3:15 the word answer is the term that means to give an *answer*, but as a lawyer would in a courtroom. Think about this analogy: The lawyer comes in and has to be cognizant of the judge. There is a jury listening who is less knowledgeable, and he has a formidable foe across the aisle listening to every participle of a sentence and scrutinizing it. He has to remember that he also has to give comfort to the one who has entrusted him to defend him. The lawyer cannot lose his cool; his presentation has to be calm. If he gets dramatic, it is dramatic only for effect. He cannot be overly angry or he will either be in contempt or he will offend the jury and they will be offended by his personality and possibly overlook the facts. In dealing with the facts, they have to be well thought out, with a very systematic approach, and very well rehearsed. He has to know the arguments, points, and counter points twelve steps into the process—well learned and well prepared.

Long gone is the response, "God said it, I believe it and that settles it". In the Scopes trials that's what branded us as uneducated. If His Word is truth, it will be able to stand the test of any examination, successfully refuting any scrutiny in examination so it is fine to put it to the test. It is much like an anvil. Many things are pounded upon it and tools may wear down, yet the anvil stands. That's the Word of God. So be systematic, be thoughtful, be well prepared, and be ready to give responses. Incidentally I have found that preparation breeds confidence, and it is healthy to be well prepared and ready to field arguments and questions and to know what principles will guide your advice.

Reason With Them

Paul reasoned with them and asked people to reason with him. I think it's very important to know that God is very aware of our life and our circumstance; just as it says in 1 Corinthians that Apollos watered and Paul preached and so on. They said they are equal. I think we ought to all share the gospel to bring a person to a decision, yet if they don't come to a decision, before God, ask them to consider the gospel again. It's okay after you've sensed a hesitation to ask them to reason and think it over. You do not want to stir their emotions for a just a response. Believe me, they may be emotionally stirred, but you do not want to stir their emotions so that you'll hear the desired words. You want their heart to be changed and there are some individuals that will have to take time to process all you have to say.

Have Restraint

Another passage that is often overlooked is 1 Corinthians 1:18. It talks about having restraint and not quickly being offended. *"For the word of the cross is foolishness to those who are perishing, but to us who are being saved it is the power of God."* Therefore in talking to someone, you have to approach the conversation with a level of restraint. Even though you know the precious truth and understand the glorious gospel, the most intelligent unbeliever cannot fully comprehend the preciousness of the gospel until the moment they are convicted to accept Christ. They can watch the movie "The Passion" and be stirred, but yet people who are unbelievers can never really know the precious treasure they are treading on. In Matt. 7:6 it says, "You will cast pearl in front of swine." Literally it is this precious jewel these animals do not even understand. They are pushing it around with their noses. They do not really understand what they are treading on at all. If you are evangelizing an unbeliever they will not know what blasphemy they are uttering. If Eph. 2:1-3 is true, then that means their entire conduct is offensive to God. In 1 Timothy Paul even regretted some of the words he himself uttered about Jesus Christ. In 1 Timothy 1:12-16 he says, *"I thank Christ Jesus our Lord, who has strengthened me, because He considered me faithful, putting me into service, even though I was formerly a blasphemer and a persecutor and a violent aggressor. Yet I was shown mercy because I acted ignorantly in unbelief; and the grace of our Lord was more than abundant, with the faith and love, which are found in Christ Jesus. It is a trustworthy statement, deserving full acceptance, that Christ Jesus came into the world to save sinners, among whom I am foremost of all. Yet for this reason I found mercy, so that in me as the foremost, Jesus Christ might demonstrate His perfect patience as an example for those who would believe in Him for eternal life."* You try to caution this individual, but if you're witnessing don't be surprised if they tread on something blasphemous if they are not a believer. You must have restraint. Unfortunately, they don't know the precious truth upon which they are treading.

Befriend Them

In 2 John 9-10, we read about how to maintain a standard of limited courtesies toward those who refuse the gospel. These verses speak to sharing the gospel with someone who is hostile to the teachings of the gospel. How do you know it is time to stop talking to those who have rejected the gospel time and time again? My advice is this: When you have said all that you can say and they know the script and they know *everything* you are going say, *and* they still remain *hostile*; then, you have done your part. Pray for them, and begin sharing with others. If, of course, they are still entertaining the discussion and have honest questions, then continue the discussion. Matthew 10:14 speaks to those who are hostile to the truth; not to those sincerely seeking, "And whosoever shall not receive you, nor hear your words, when you depart out of that house or city, shake off the dust of your feet." Likewise, Acts 13:50-51, "But the Jews stirred up the devout and prominent women and the chief men of the city, raised up persecution against Paul and Barnabas, and expelled them from their region. But they shook off the dust from their feet against them, and came to Iconium."

Also notice that this verse says not to bid them "godspeed" (KJV). This term means that you should not extend to hostile unbelievers the small and seemingly insignificant accolades that we often extend to other believers. For example, to believers, I will personally end an email with a phrase like "God Bless" then type my name. But when I know that I am emailing an unbeliever, I will politely conclude the email with "Sincerely" or "Hope you have a great day." To share meaningful spiritual encouragements with unbelievers may very well make them content with how they are spiritually – all the while they remain lost and in their sinful state. 2 John 9-10 teaches that until they accept what you share, there is still a distinction between all who are saved and those who are lost.

Take Time To Listen

It is so important that we take time to not only rehearse what the specific and necessary biblical truths are so that we will be biblically accurate, but that we take time with the same level of scrutiny to assess and listen to the life situation of the person so that we can measure what words will minister most effectively to the heart of the one receiving the message of the Gospel. After rehearsing all of these biblical principles related to tact, people skills, and the means by which to share these principles in this chapter, I am reminded of the time tested, universal teachings that the Bible provides for you and me that encourage us to be mindful of the life story of those we meet. For example, Colossians 4:5 comes to mind where it encourages us, *"Conduct yourselves with wisdom toward outsiders, making the most of the opportunity."* Another verse that encourages us to use various approaches for different personalities is I Thessalonians 5:14, *"We urge you, brethren, admonish the unruly, encourage the fainthearted, help the weak, be patient with everyone."*

Think about all the people in your life who have framed their words just so in order to help you understand a concept, the error of your ways, a soft correction or tender rebuke, and have done it such a way to where in their thoughtfulness and consideration of you framed their words so that you left encouraged as well! They helped turn what could have been a horrible, painful memory into a time of learning, growing, and thankfulness. We are blessed to have these people in our lives, and we can be a blessing in return as we continue presenting the biggest love story to the world in the same spirit.

write It Down

Recall the last time you shared the message of salvation with someone. Were you ready? What were some questions that they asked you, that if prepared you could have answered better? How did the conversation end?

_____

_____

_____

_____

_____

_____

_____

_____

_____

_____

_____

_____

_____

_____

_____

Take some time to think about those you know who are need of salvation. Who are they? Write their names down. Pray for them. What can you do to move your relationship into one that welcomes sharing the gospel?

_____

_____

_____

_____

_____

_____

_____

_____

_____

_____

_____

_____

_____

_____

_____

_____

_____

_____

Notes

Three Is Enough

We have spent some time discussing how to enter into an intimate relationship with Jesus Christ, how to cultivate and maintain that intimacy throughout our lives, and how to share the wonderful story of His grace and love with others. But I would be remiss if I didn't share one final thought with you in order to round out this entire spiritual discussion. I need to answer the question, "So, how do I practically live out all of these principles in my day-to-day life?"

Just like a lecture that fails to explain how the teachings of the discipline can be integrated into the real world , or like a pastor, who after he elucidates the most acute, profound points of a theological doctrine, fails to show how the profound truth is able to affect the daily lives of the parishioner, I would consider this book incomplete if I didn't take the time to provide for you some very practical recommendations for living out the principles in this book on a day-to-day basis.

Here are some practical suggestions on how you can live out the spiritual teachings found in this book. Practice them regularly. Remain sensitive to the Holy Spirit's guidance on how to pray during your practice of these spiritual activities. And be careful to never forget that you need to be performing these activities with your whole heart, not simply mechanically checking them off your list.

KNOW

Try solidifying the teachings in chapters one and two in your mind by asking a believing friend to pose some questions, as if he or she is an unbeliever who is sincerely seeking to know what the Bible says about the truth of salvation in Jesus Christ. Here are some questions you should be prepared to answer, and assume that after every question your friend will follow up with this question, "How do you know that?" This will make you have to understand the Bible references that you quote to your friend when responding to the initial question:

1. Why do I need to be saved?
2. Is everyone in need of salvation?
3. Can I save myself?
4. Can I approach God assuming that he will give me – a nice, respectful person – a "pass" and not hold me to the same level of spiritual scrutiny that He holds other people to?
5. What is God's role in saving my soul?
6. Is everyone automatically saved since Jesus died and rose again?
7. Is having a cognitive knowledge of all the truths presented in chapter one enough to be saved?
8. What is the difference between "cognitive" knowledge and "volitional" knowledge of these saving truths?
9. Create your own additional questions that you believe would help you retain and comprehend all the teachings in these chapters.

Now, turn the tables and you play the role of the inquiring unbeliever and have your friend respond to these questions. You may think that your friend has it easier because he/she just heard your response, but this is not always the case. Knowing the concept, and hearing the concept audibly is one thing, but speaking out the concept to a friend in a clear, concise fashion is very challenging.

When you have the teachings understood fairly well, you ought to prepare a mini salvation presentation. Meaning, pretend that you are walking in a parking lot and meet a friend, coworker, or colleague. You find yourself walking together into the building. You both walk through the lobby and approach the elevator. You have approximately twelve floors to go up and it is only you two. Right as you enter the elevator, your colleague, knowing you are a Christian, asks you, "Hey, could you tell me what it means to be saved?" Knowing that as soon as the elevator door opens on the Twelfth Floor you both will have to immediately engage in your work, meetings, phone calls, and work-related conversations so you figure you will only have approximately 45-60 seconds to share the gospel. This is indeed the time you'll need to present your previously prepared, mini salvation presentation. Here are some suggestions:

1. Write out the essential elements of the presentation that absolutely must be known by a person in order to be saved.
2. Decide what can be discussed in a follow-up conversation. That is, decide what details are not essential to the salvation presentation but could be held over because you would be getting too far ahead of yourself and confuse the issue.
3. Rehearse this presentation with a friend. The goal is to have well-prepared, well-thought-out, sincere presentation.

4. Go out with a friend and look for 45-60 second opportunities. I know that may sound strange but remember, in today's society time is precious and people are not normally going to make a major decision in 45-60 seconds. Look at this as a first step in the witnessing process. Others will water and God will bring the increase. Who knows, 45 seconds may turn into 45 minutes and God may provide you with the incredible blessing of seeing a spiritual miracle occur right in front of your eyes!

5. Now, for the biggest challenge, convert this 45-60 second presentation into the language of a six year old without skewing or omitting any truth. Be vivid, imaginative, patient, and very prepared. Consider it a victory if they are able to grasp only one piece of the salvation puzzle during your conversation. Rehearse this a few times introducing new information each time until it becomes natural and you are at ease with it and God will use it to illuminate the mind by the work of the Spirit in another person's soul.

You will find that this practice works on adults as well. A simple, well-thought-out, well-prepared presentation will hold their interest. As a lecturer, I have never understood why we adults have made instructional times so boring. I think you will find that a child-like presentation works for adults when it comes to the salvation message.

In addition to these activities, go back and rehearse your own personal thoughts and reflections that you wrote down in the "Write it down" section at the end of Chapter Two. As the Apostle John encourages us in Revelation 2:5, "remember from where you came," it is good to dwell, not on the sin and damage done, but on the miraculous delivery God has provided in our lives. And there is no greater deliverance than that of God's salvation of our souls.

Walk Close

Based on the teaching of the parable regarding the shepherd who had 100 sheep, in your own heart recall the moments in your life that you have no doubt in your mind that God used "to break your leg," to turn you off a path of sin and protect you from a life of deep regret. Take a moment to thank the Lord through prayer and thank the Lord for taking you off that path. Talk to the Lord and tell Him how things are going now in your life. Have you gotten back on the same path of sin or are you following a path of righteousness now? If you are on the same path of sin, confess immediately and passionately to God and commit to pursue righteousness.

In addition, find a friend or two who are committed to pursue righteousness in the very little things of life and surround yourself with them so that you will be encouraged to honor the Lord in every area of your life. Engage in spiritual discussions with them. Talk about the scriptures with them. Pray with them. Worship with them. Socialize with them. And, remember, even strong Christians are still human and will make mistakes and poor choices. So, if someone lets you down spiritually, remember that your hope is not in a person, but your hope and encouragement is found in the Lord. Remember, it comes down to your own commitment, passion, and love for the Lord Jesus Christ, and you must be willing to allow the Holy Spirit to guide your life.

Based on the teaching of the parable regarding the woman who had 10 coins, would an onlooker know by your conduct and character that you are indeed a Christian. Go through your past week (at work, school, the gym, after hours, in the mornings, on the athletic field, etc.) and ask yourself if your interactions, decisions, attitude, words, body language, framing of emails, responses, failure to respond, etc. caused others around you to think positively of you. More so, did your actions point others to the fact that you are a Christian and foster comments from them like, "you did not react like other people would have reacted," "thank you for being so kind," "boy, the others took the news a totally different way," or, "you acted differently?" If you were able to point to positive experiences, then take a moment to thank God for the opportunity to spread the goodness of God through your actions and ask Him if He would give you more opportunities to testify of His goodness through your actions. If you realized that you had not demonstrated a Christ-like spirit during your past week, take a moment to apologize to Jesus for not being a strong, effective witness of His goodness, identify the sin(s) that you are harboring that keep you feeling that you have every right to act or feel in the non-Christian way you did, then ask the Lord for an opportunity to testify of God's goodness this coming week – as a way to show Him that you are serious about your commitment to look like a true believer in your everyday walk.

Based on the teaching of the parable regarding the father who had two sons, take time to reflect on when the Lord gave you a second chance. Consider the people in your life who showed you the mercy of the Lord and made it possible for you to get back up again spiritually. Think about the words they used and the amount of time they took to talk to you about getting on the right path. Consider the time commitment and emotional battle that took place in their hearts to confront you regarding your sin. As you do, thank God for their courage, love, and commitment to your well being. Ask yourself how their actions reflect the last two verses of the Book of James (5:19-20) and how their commitment to you reflected these two verses. In addition, consider how their actions kept a multitude of sins from occurring in your life and take a moment to thank God for that encounter, and if possible, thank them again.

Try taking some time to analyze and discuss a recent sermon from your pastor and/or a teaching lesson that you and your friends had recently heard, and discuss if the lesson or sermon was directed to unbelievers, believers, or both. What was said or not said that made you come to this conclusion? If it's both, how do you think the unbelieving attendees received the sermon? Would they have understood the teaching of the gospel clearly or was it too veiled? What could have been included to make the presentation clearer for the unbelievers to understand the gospel presentation? Remember, when you analyze and critique a sermon or a teaching lesson, you should ALWAYS be positive and supportive of the one who proclaimed the truth, and realize that not every sermon has to speak to both believers and unbelievers. Never forget that the Lord leads presenters of the gospel to direct their comments in one way or another so do not be quick to conclude that a particular sermon was imbalanced if it did not speak to both believers and unbelievers. Simply do this exercise as an observation exercise.

Search the scriptures to see if there is another teaching lesson by Jesus and/or the apostles that was directed both to believers and unbelievers. The Gospels (Matthew, Mark, Luke, John) and the Book of Acts may be a good place to look for teaching lessons from Jesus and/or the apostles. Discuss the components that you believe were directed to believers and which components of the teaching were directed to unbelievers. After you discuss some of these passages with a friend or two, possibly think about how you would share one of these passages with a mixed audience of believers and unbelievers. What would the title of your talk be? What points would you emphasize? How would you wrap up your teaching lesson? Note: A good source to guide you may be your pastor or someone who has had experience juggling the dynamics of a multi-interest audience.

Walk Guarded

Reflect once again on your own personal thoughts and reflections that you wrote down in the "Write it down" section at the end of Chapter Four. The truths you were asked to ponder in this section are especially thought provoking as they cause you to search deep down in your heart and ask some serious spiritual questions. Doing this exercise is necessary and the most important spiritual exercise of this chapter.

Begin praying every single morning – without fail – the words that I pray myself, "Lord, as I start my day with You, please keep me sensitive to the very baby steps of sin. Make me be able to sense when I am beginning down this digression of sin. And if so, give me the wisdom to turn and run toward You in honesty, confession, and a love for You and Your righteousness. I want righteousness to dictate terms in my life today!" Now, when I find myself having to confess to God that I had been insensitive to the baby steps of sin on that particular day, I make sure I pray this prayer to Him once again. The point being, make sure you are in constant communion with the Lord regarding your spiritual challenges so that you catch your sin early before it permeates your entire heart and mind.

Begin a brief search of the scriptures that speak to God providing victory over sin. After you find these scriptures, call a friend and share the verse(s) with him/her. Ask them to share their thoughts, then pray together and ask the Lord to give you the wisdom to obey Him so that you will always experience victory in your own life. After you do this, commit to memorize a verse at a time then ask God to provide the opportunity for you to share the truth of these verses with another person who may be in need of hearing about how he/she can experience God's victory. Repeat this process throughout the coming days, weeks, and months. This type of spiritual activity is the purest form of providing spiritual edification to our fellow brothers and sisters in Christ.

Building on the previous recommended spiritual activity, I want to encourage you to embark on what may initially sound like a scary endeavor; that is, I want you to take one of the verses that you find in your research and begin preparing to teach both the meaning and application of it to someone else. Let me pause here and explain what I mean by teach. Don't always default to thinking of a pastor or professor when you think about being taught. When you teach someone something, it often is done outside of a classroom or pulpit, but is done as you are living life together. Teaching occurs when you give advice while sipping coffee on a park bench, while you walk down a sidewalk pushing the stroller with a friend and his/her infant, while you are sitting in a softball team's dugout waiting to take the field, etc. Anywhere you find a person elaborating on what a portion of scripture means and how it can apply to their life is teaching. In fact, having these discussions as you are living life with a friend is the essence of teaching. So, I want you to focus on a verse, study what it says, do a little more digging by reading the surrounding context of the verse in the chapter of the Bible that it is found in, then search out an occasion to teach it to someone else. I would recommend that you ask a friend if you can try your thoughts out on them to see if they are clear and understandable. I think you will find their questions will help you know what aspects of the verse need to be presented more clearly. Receiving his/her feedback will also tip you off to what is important to the listener and most likely future audiences. After you share it with your friend, consider their feedback, and find another person to share your thoughts with in a casual way regarding the passage.

Walking In Grace

Just like in the previous chapter, it would be very helpful to begin by reflecting on your own personal thoughts and reflections that you wrote down in the "Write it down" section at the end of Chapter Five. Now, further your thoughts on what is needed to take you back to a healthy spiritual state by focusing on James, Chapter 5. Begin to list very practical things that can be done every day of your week to strengthen you to return to a healthy spiritually state. Then ask a very close, trustworthy, honest friend who demonstrates personal holiness for their opinion on what you wrote down and to possibly add other spiritual activities to your list.

Also pick a few friends and to have varying levels of spiritual conversation with. Some friends may be friends that you have encouraging spiritual discussion with over coffee and breakfast to start your day on Monday morning. The conversation may simply be about what God did yesterday in the Sunday morning service. You can discuss the spiritual results that came from the preaching and ministry of your church, reflecting on the ways God is at work in the lives of other people. These types of conversations can occur any time of the week and are often casual, friendly, and very exciting. Additional conversations you could have would be with friends who are passionate about similar areas of ministry that you have. You could spend time discussing what more could be done to best minister to your area of focus in your congregation. You could rehearse what produced spiritual growth in the past and what can be done to continue to solidify spiritual decisions made. Make a conscience effort to remember to praise God for all He has done and is doing in the lives of people.

Lastly, take some time to begin brief, friendly conversations with Christians in your church, workplace, and home, and ask them what is exciting them about what God is doing in their life. "Is he teaching you anything this month about Himself?" "Has God given you guidance regarding any decisions you were praying to Him about in this last month?" "Have you had (or heard of) any prayer requests that have been answered by God in the last month? If so, what were they and how did God answer the request? Did He answer in the way you thought He would?" Of course, after every question, ask "How can all that I am talking about apply to me?" "How can I take what I have just heard testified about God's guidance, power, and goodness and inculcate it in my heart, life, and practice?"

It is important to continue this practice of having intentional, spiritual discussion with other believers. It is this rehearsing of spiritual truth that revives our soul, informs our worship, and makes our minds not only well versed in the scriptures but also crave spiritual things. If you string enough spiritual discussions together, you will find that you do not want to go a day without engaging other believers in these types of discussions.

Serve Others

This chapter would be great for group discussion. It contains a lot of points that tend to be of interest to many believers. I only wish I could attend some of your discussion groups as you process the spiritual teachings presented in this chapter. Here are some leading questions I encourage you to discuss:

> 1. If you would have been asked, "What is a Godly Person?" how would you have responded?

> 2. What was your initial thought when you read that there is a difference between a mere Christian and a godly Christian? Possibly consider Galatians 6:1 where it describes how the church ought to choose certain believers out of a congregation to keep a fallen believer accountable.

> 3. What is your opinion of the definition of a godly person being one who is self-disciplined in godly attitudes and habits?

> 4. Prayerfully ask everyone in the group if they are indeed a godly person. Have a time of prayer so that your discussion group members can ask the Lord to forgive them and/or thank Him for His power to become a godly person once again.

Read Psalm 139 per the basic outline that I provided in Chapter Six. This time, take time to stop and pause at the end of each section to reflect on the details of God's immutable attributes (omniscience, omnipresence, and omnipotence). Spend one session on each division of this Psalm if necessary to ponder the vastness of the greatness of our God. Then take time to comprehend the great care that the Psalmist took to tell God that he wanted to be looked upon as different from anyone who finds it easy to blaspheme the Lord. Ask yourself if you do all you can do to make sure that you are far removed from anything that would cause people to think that you do not honor the Lord Jesus Christ. Think of little things you could do that would make a tactful statement to all that you are indeed *different.*

Consider the teaching of John 14:1-3 and ask the very simple question, "Am I a faithful Bride?" This question could go two ways in your life. I would encourage you to identify what you believe you are doing that the Lord is indeed pleased with. I know this may be somewhat uncomfortable for some because you actually will be articulating things that you believe you are doing right before the Lord. But don't feel that you are being prideful or arrogant; rather maybe preface your statements with these words, "Lord, thank you for giving me the wisdom to see what I need to do. Keep me close to you and I will strive to remain obedient to You." Remember, as a Father, our Lord longs to hear of the obedience of His children and longs to bless His children immensely. Also, identify what areas of your life you could improve on so that you are always living as a faithful bride. As you do this, pray to the Lord – the One Who both loves you and desires the absolute best for you – and tell Him why you think you have been tempted to disobey Him in an area of your life. Confess to Him that you are sorry and that you regret giving in to those passions. Then, begin to tell Him what you will do for the remainder of the day to safeguard your heart and mind from considering being unfaithful to Him.

Don't try to gain spiritual victory in one all-encompassing action or activity. You did not just fall into sin all of a sudden nor will the recovery back to a strong state require only one magical action or activity. You need to take baby steps in your spiritual walk – one day at a time. Create little and numerous spiritual victories in your life. Take time to praise the Lord and celebrate these times of obedience by talking with a friend and let them know that, "Hey, I made it through another day" or "We had a good time focusing on spiritual things to-night and my mind was focused more than it has ever been in a long time," etc. So, make a list of what seem to be "little spiritual victories" that you would be able to celebrate and praise the Lord for. Consider if there are daily victories, half-day victories, even hourly victories. I believe this ability of seeing progress and experiencing victories will encourage you not to throw away all that the Spirit has done and is obviously doing in your life to keep you faithful to Him!

Share with others

Building on what we practiced in Chapters One and Two, begin now to prepare for a longer presentation of the gospel lasting 4-7 minutes. Take what you have learned in Chapter Seven and begin working on a well-framed, systematic, well-thought-out presentation of the gospel. Prepare a presentation for a receptive seeker whi is kind, courteous, and willing to listen. Be prepared for questions that may not relate to what you are trying to share. Also be prepared for some-one who may have a hostile reaction and who wants to argue. Remember, what dispels fear is confidence in God and a well-prepared presentation.

Again, build on what we practiced in Chapters One and Two, rather than have a random encounter with a stranger. Take a moment to think of someone spe-cifically who is in need of hearing the gospel message. Begin praying for this person by name. Tell the Lord how you feel about this person and why you chose his/her name. Tell the Lord how you feel about sharing the Gospel to him/her. Are you scared? Nervous? Excited? Impatient? Happy? Sad? Then articulate to God exactly why you feel this way. Rehearse the teachings that you learned in Chapters One, Two, and Seven and see if these verses provide the knowledge that you need in order to overcome your fears. Of course,

Chapters One and Two provide the Bible's teaching on what salvation is and is not. Chapter Seven encourages you to be prepared in many ways as you share these truths with others. So, the only remaining fear is possibly, "What if they ask me a question that is not addressed in this book?" Then your answer is either, "Well, good question. I don't know that question right now, but I know there is a reasonable answer that supports the Bible's teaching about salvation; so, if you would allow me a little time, I am going to ask someone who may know and/or find a writing that deals with these questions and then get back with you." Remember, unless you are a scholar with a Ph.D. in every academic field of discipline, you are bound to say, "I don't know" a few million times in your lifetime. There is no shame in not knowing how to respond immediately.

Simply make a list of questions and then tell them that you will research the answer and get back to them. But be quick to ask them a question in return, "If I take the time to research the issue, and I return to you with a response that supports the Bible and its teaching about salvation, will you then believe that the Bible is true and give your heart to Jesus Christ?" Of course, if someone is not sincere, they will shrug this off and raise give other excuses as to why they do not believe – and that shows you that regardless, their heart is set on not believing in Jesus Christ. But the sincere ones will realize that they will have to be put to a point of decision if you return with sound answers to their questions. Remember also that when you are witnessing and being kind and respectful as Chapter Seven teaches, you are not the only one who has to answer questions. It is also incumbent upon the one to whom you are witnessing to respond to your questions as well. So ask them a lot of questions. Make them tell you what they believe about salvation. Ask them follow up questions like, "So, according to your way, I could work for my own salvation. So, how do I know when I have done enough good things? Who makes this judgment call? Do other imperfect humans decide this?" Or a line of questioning like, "If peace is found within ourselves, how do I know I am always right and guiding myself down a healthy path? Do I know if my path is perfect until I become perfect and all-knowing? Has anyone ever reached that goal of perfection? If so, should we then begin to consult him/her? Ask questions of the ones you are witnessing to and listen to them. Then after you have asked them questions and listened to them, ask them more questions about their beliefs and listen some more. You may find that the more they rehearse their belief system the more they realize the gaping holes in it.

After Three

I have heard it said that, "Practice does not make perfect. Practice only makes permanent. Perfect practice makes perfect." The spiritual activities presented in this final chapter are for the purpose of spurring you on to practice what you have learned in this book. Of course, there are many more activities and ideas that would help you solidify these teachings in your heart. So, I encourage you to think of more ways – unique ways – that you believe would honor the Lord, protect the pure gospel message, and be effective in reaching others with the saving knowledge of Jesus Christ. My deepest heart's cry for you as a believer in Jesus Christ is for you to know the Lord more intimately, testify of His saving grace, love, and mercy to those around you, and for you to be a walking example of holiness, righteousness, and purity before those who are observing you and looking up to you for a spiritual example by which to model their own lives. Life is too short and God's truth too precious to keep His message contained within us or to squander our testimony by pursuing sin. Even though my heart desires to join each and every one of you at your churches, ministries, and missions, and to worship with you, rehearsing these wonderful truths together, my only request is that you make a lifetime commitment to purpose in your heart to live out the words of the Apostle Paul:

"Dear friends, you always followed my instructions when I was with you. And now that I am away, it is even more important. Work hard to show the results of your salvation, obeying God with deep reverence and fear. For God is working in you, giving you the desire and the power to do what pleases him."
- Philippians 2:12-13 NLT